Sensational Stars

by
Gail Garber

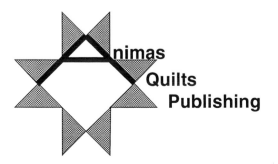

nimas
Quilts
Publishing

600 Main Ave.
Durango, CO. 81301
(970) 247-2582

Sensational Stars

Animas Quilts Publishing
600 Main Ave.
Durango, CO. 81301
(970) 247-2582

ISBN: 1-885156-14-6

Printed on Recycled Paper

Cover Quilt:
  Star Radiance, 96" x 96"
  by Helen Duncan
  Albuquerque, New Mexico

Back Cover:
  Starry, Starry Night, 80" x 80"
  by Gail Garber
  Rio Rancho, New Mexico

CREDITS:

Editor	Kim Gjere
Graphics	Jackie Robinson
	Gail Garber
Photography	Christopher Marona

Printed in Colorado

ABOUT THE AUTHOR

Gail began quilting in 1980, after sewing since a teenager. Her first quilting class definitely changed the sewing direction of her life. She discovered the endless design possibilities and color combinations of quilts and was no longer interested in other types of sewing.

She began teaching in 1983 and published her first quilting pattern, "Apache Canyon," in 1988. Gail has a line of quilting and clothing patterns, and teaches and lectures throughout the world.

In her other life, Gail is the Executive Director of a non-profit organization, Hawks Aloft. They work to conserve birds of prey and other wildlife through research and education programs. She also houses some of the permanently injured, non-releasable, educational raptors in large outdoor flights in her backyard.

For information about Gail Garber Designs, send a LSASE to: P.O. Box 10028, Albuquerque, NM 87184, (505) 892-3354.

ACKNOWLEDGEMENTS

The women who made quilts for the book were an inspiration to work with and encouraging throughout the process: Helen Duncan, Susie Gray, Linnie Hyde, Sharon Johnson, Darlene Jones, Anita McSorley, Harriet Smith, and Janet Wolfe. Ann Silva's Bernina Sewing Center generously donated classroom space. Donna Barnitz and Jean Sinclair helped test patterns and text and offered good-natured moral support. Lynn Graves, a brainstorming genius and long-time friend, also made possible a quilting retreat at her cabin.

BIBLIOGRAPHY

Beyer, Jinny. *The Quilter's Album of Blocks and Borders.* McLean, VA: EPM Publications, 1980.

Hargrave, Harriet. *Heirloom Machine Quilting.* Lafayette, CA: C & T Publishing, 1995.

Mathieson, Judy. *Mariner's Compass, An American Quilt Classic.* Lafayette, CA: C & T Publishing, 1987.

Miller, Margaret. *Blockbuster Quilts.* Botthel, WA: That Patchwork Place, 1991.

Noble, Maurine. *Machine Quilting Made Easy.* Botthel, WA: That Patchwork Place, 1994.

Pasquini, Katie. *Mandala.* Eureka, CA: Sudz Publishing, 1983.

Rocke, Lora. *Easy Traditional Quilting.* Durango, CO: Animas Quilts Publishing, 1995.

TABLE OF CONTENTS

INTRODUCTION

My interest in star quilts began in 1983 when I saw a photo of a famous quilt, "Ray of Light Medallion" by Jinny Beyer. It was the most beautiful quilt I had ever seen. I suspected that there was no way in the world to buy a quilt that wonderful, so I set about learning how to make my own. In 1984, I joined a quilt group to explore medallion quilt design. Under the tutelage of quiltmaker Ruby Chick, I embarked on the journey that lead to this book.

We learned to design, draft, and hand stitch medallion quilts. My quilt, Azimuth, an archaic word for compass, remains one of my favorites. It has traveled around the world, been featured in many publications, and won several awards.

During this time my skills in other areas improved, especially machine piecing. I read a book by Judy Mathieson, "Mariner's Compass". This book gives the quilter confidence to piece these designs on the sewing machine. I learned that machine piecing was not only possible, it was considerably easier and more accurate than hand piecing.

I began changing the traditional compass design, a circle that has been cut into pie-shaped wedges. I treated each wedge as a separate piece, working on design elements within that shape.

About the same time I began teaching quilting classes. A favorite was a block of the month. The Star Block of the Month Class began in January of 1994. When it became apparent that these stars might form the basis for a book, I approached the class with the idea of forming an additional group. This group would focus on original designs and settings.

Eight women accepted the challenge. Their quilts are featured in the book. All have some blocks in common, yet none of their quilts are alike.

This book will guide you through the process of designing your own blocks and settings for a unique quilt. Or, if you prefer, start out by making one of the quilts featured. Read all of the general directions before beginning your project.

GENERAL DIRECTIONS

EQUIPMENT

The correct equipment, in good working order, makes all the difference in the world when it comes to success in making a project. I hear from my students and have personally experienced the joy of seeing my sewing skills increase immeasurably upon getting a new, high-quality sewing machine. In addition to a sewing machine you'll need the following supplies.

Drafting Supplies - To draft your own design.

1. High quality compass - Use a professional drafting compass with an extension arm. These compasses have screws which hold them in position and the extension arm allows you to draw circles as large as 14". The small ones designed for school use slip during the drawing process and are not accurate.

2. Protractor - A protractor is used for accurately measuring angles. My favorite is cut from one piece of plastic with no hole in the center. This makes it more stable.

3. Mechanical pencil - These give a finer line than standard pencils.

4. Eraser - Art gum erasers erase completely and quickly.

5. Large paper - Graph paper is not necessary, since the lines drawn generally do not correspond with those on graph paper. Standard newsprint (unprinted, of course) is fine or you may purchase pads of large-size drawing paper.

6. An 18" see-thru ruler - These are necessary for drawing the basic lines and for adding the 1/4" seam allowance to the templates.

Always check the ruler for accuracy. The printed lines on a ruler are often printed slightly to one side. You may find that one side has a perfect quarter inch while the other side is slightly larger. If this is the case, mark the "good" side so that it is easily identifiable. Also check the ends of the ruler for accuracy.

All rulers are not created equal. Make sure that those used in a project have consistent measurements. Whenever possible, use the same ruler throughout a project.

7. A 12" or 16" square ruler - This valuable tool helps create perfect squares which are a must for success. I also lay my star pieces out on the 16" ruler so I can easily see their correct arrangement when sewing. It is also convenient for carrying pieces back and forth from the ironing board to the sewing machine.

General Supplies

1. Rotary cutting supplies - You'll need a rotary cutter, mat and ruler.

2. Four inch square ruler - This rotary cutting ruler assists in cutting around small templates. Its small size makes it easy to maneuver when cutting fabric.

3. Neutral color thread - Because you constantly stitch over different colors of fabric, a medium gray thread blends with most colors. I recommend using high quality cotton sewing threads. Thread sold for several spools per dollar is less durable and often breaks during sewing.

4. White double-napped flannel - A two yard piece pinned to a wall makes a quick, easy, and portable flannel board. Cotton adheres to flannel. I like to stick my cut pieces to the flannel, and then step back and view the star before stitching.

Other Supplies - Helpful but not essential.

1. A quarter inch presser foot - These feet are 1/4" wide from the center needle position to the right side of the foot.

2. Compass points - These are movable points which fit a 1" wide ruler or yardstick. They are used for drawing circles as large as 70".

3. 3-M Spray Mount™ Artist's Adhesive - This is a re-stickable spray glue, similar to that found on Post-it™ notes, used for making templates and transferring quilting designs. I do not recommend permanent spray glues.

4. Pen/pencil adaptor for compasses - This small tool attaches a mechanical pencil to the drawing end of the compass.

FABRIC SELECTION AND YARDAGE

Choosing Fabric

Everyone has individual likes and dislikes. Because of these differences, there is no easy, magic formula which will work for everyone.

I like to begin by choosing one fabric, and then select others that complement it. A well-balanced quilt will have a blend of colors, color values, and textures. For a sampler type quilt, I generally use 1-2 focal fabrics, 8-10 accent (or coordinating) fabrics, 1-2 background fabrics, and sometimes a zinger.

Focal Fabric - These often have several colors within the same print and can be either large or medium in scale. They may be floral, geometric, or simple swirls of colors. These fabrics are often the basis for a quilt, because you can simply choose other fabrics based on the colors in the focal print. Begin with one of these prints. You may use greater amounts of focal fabric because it will be used in several blocks and possibly the setting or borders. Because a focal fabric is often a large print, the design may repeat less often than a small print.

TIP - Fussy cutting or isolating a print creates wonderful circular designs in an area where several identical templates meet, as in the center of a star. To achieve this effect, isolate one part of a print or a stripe, cutting each template from the same exact portion of the print. For instance, if you isolate a leaf which swirls to the left, with a hint of color at one end, you will need to cut each of the templates from the exact same leaf. You'll love the effect. Plan on buying extra fabric since fussy cutting uses a large amount of fabric.

Color Value - A successful quilt will have a combination of light, medium, and dark colors. These can be either prints or solids. Avoid selecting colors that coordinate too closely. From a distance these all appear to be the same fabric.

Texture - Again, avoid careful coordination of fabrics. Choose a variety of textures. This means small, medium and large prints with differing scales. Quilts which include the same size and texture prints may appear to be plain, even with a good blend of colors.

Solids - Wonderfully colorful quilts can be made entirely with solid color fabrics. Close attention to color placement, contrast, and color value are necessary. Solids can also be used as accent fabrics or for textural contrast with other prints.

Accent Fabrics - These are fabrics which more or less coordinate with the focal fabric. Choose several.

A Zinger - This is one fabric which doesn't match the others in your quilt - at least not perfectly! It may be from the opposite side of the color wheel such as a burst of orange in an otherwise lavender and purple quilt. Zingers add interest.

Quality Fabrics - The process of making a quilt may take anywhere from 40 to 1,000 hours of careful planning and stitching. Your work will be enhanced and the project more enjoyable if you use fine quality fabric. Quilt shops cater to your needs and have a wide range of cottons in every hue imaginable. They buy better quality and a wider range of fabrics that make wonderful quilts. Quilt shops also provide assistance with figuring yardage, help with fabric selection, and the latest tips and techniques to make your project successful.

How Much Fabric to Buy?

Perhaps this is the most difficult of all questions and the one that is most frequently asked. Again there is no easy answer, except that you should buy more than you think you will need. Invariably, the fabric you have the least of will become your favorite somewhere in the process of making your quilt.

First, decide on the size of your quilt and how many blocks you will use. Each block will differ in the number of prints used and the amount of fabric needed. For each block you will need approximately:

One - 14" square of background fabric (a fat quarter)
1/8 yard of focal fabric or stripe
1/8 yard each of 3-5 coordinating fabrics.

Remember, while you will use only 3-5 different fabrics for each block, you will need 8-10 different accent fabrics for the whole quilt.

While these are somewhat generous measurements, they are useful when determining how much to buy for the entire quilt. Extra fabric allows you to make choices during the quiltmaking process. It is always better to have too much fabric than not enough. Consult the chart in the next column to determine approximate amounts of fabric. Use this table only for *estimating* the amount of fabric to be used in *blocks*, not the entire quilt.

NOTE: You may choose to use more than one background fabric. The background yardage in the chart is generous to enable you to use this fabric for borders or setting blocks together.

4-Block Quilt
 1/2 yd. Focal
 1/4 yd. each 3-5 Accents
 1 yd. Background

9-Block Quilt
 3/4 yd. Focal
 1/4 yd. each 6-8 Accents
 2 yds. Background

12-Block Quilt
 1-1/2 yds. Focal
 1/4 yd. each 7-9 Accents
 2-1/2 yds. Background

16-Block Quilt
 2 yds. Focal
 1/4 yd. each 8-10 Accents
 3 yds. Background

20-Block Quilt
 2-1/2 yds. Focal
 3/8 yd. each 8-10 Accents
 3-1/2 yds. Background

25-Block Quilt
 3 yds. Focal
 1/2 yd. each 8-10 Accents
 4 yds. Background

30-Block Quilt
 3-3/4 yds. Focal
 3/4 yds. each 8-10 Accents
 4-1/2 yds. Background

Sashing, Setting, and Borders

It is necessary to decide on the type of settings and the finished size of your quilt before you can determine how much to buy. In a sampler quilt, I frequently make all my blocks before deciding how to put them together. Refer to the sections on settings and sashings for more information.

DRAFTING STARS

Creating original star blocks is much easier than you might think. Before beginning, mentally let go of any predetermined notions about what the finished block will look like. This will enable you to concentrate on each step, one at a time, without worrying about what will happen further along.

It's always a good idea to make several practice drawings to develop an understanding for the process before drawing a full size pattern. I like to design practice blocks that measure 6" in diameter. Any that turn out well can easily be enlarged to a 12" or an 18" block. Also, the 6" block can be drawn on a standard 8-1/2" x 11" sheet of paper.

It is not necessary to use graph paper for designing star blocks because most lines drawn will not correspond to the grid. Often the grid on graph paper is not perfectly square. If you rely on paper like this it can distort your design, making it impossible to create perfect templates.

Definition Diagrams - These diagrams illustrate some of the words and angles used in this chapter.

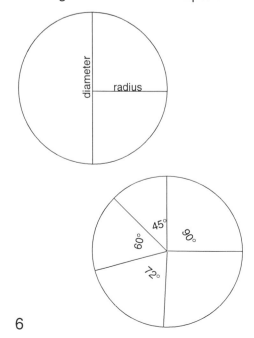

Practice Drawing - Use a ruler, compass, and protractor.

1. Begin by making a dot in the center of the piece of paper. Draw a line that is the length of the diameter of the circle, which also passes through the center dot. The dot should be in the center of the line. For example: If the finished circle will measure 6", there should be 3" on each side of the dot.

2. Place the point of the compass on the center dot. Open the compass so the pencil point reaches the end of the line, or 3". I find it is more accurate to draw measurements on paper and use them for determining how wide to open the compass. Draw the circle around the center dot.

TIP - Use a large Olfa® Cutting Mat (the smooth green one) when drawing with a compass. This makes a nice, non-slip surface to stick the point of the compass in.

3. Decide how many wedges (pie shapes) to use in the star. You can use any number but the design will be easier to draw and piece if you choose a number that divides evenly into 360°. Divide 360° by the number of wedges in the star. For example: If the star has eight wedges, then the angle of each wedge is 45°; six wedges are 60°; five wedges are 72°; etc. Use a protractor to mark points that divide the circle into the necessary number of wedges. Then draw lines that extend from the center of the circle to the outside edge.

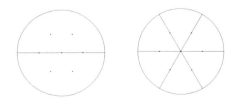

Caution: It is essential that you mark accurately. Measure each wedge to make sure that it is the correct measurement.

4. Use a protractor to mark points on the outer circle that are half way between the two sides of the wedge. These points make valuable options for adding more points to a wedge without dividing the circle into more sections.

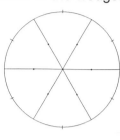

5. Now the fun part begins. Look at one wedge and think about drawing a line from one point to another. For practice purposes, let's say you want to draw a line from the halfway point of a wedge to the outside edge. First, measure a point that is 1/4 of the diameter. If your circle measures 6", then this measurement will be 1-1/2". Open the compass to that measurement and very lightly draw a circle. This easily marks the same point on each wedge.

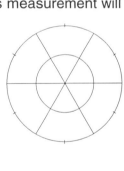

6. Draw a line from the halfway point on the outside circle to the outer corner of the wedge on the inside circle. Next draw a line from the halfway point to the outer corner on the opposite side of the wedge.

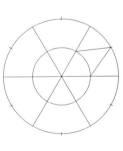

7. Look at the lines just drawn. If you like them, then draw the same lines in the remaining wedges. After completing all the lines, erase the smaller circle. Keep your work clean by erasing unnecessary lines. This

enables you to clearly view the star design as it develops.

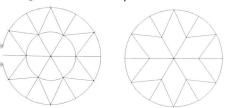

3. Draw a line across the widest part of the star point, where the circle once was. This will be easier to piece than setting in a circular center. Always simplify the drawing whenever possible.

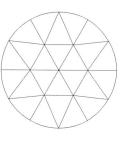

9. Look at the design and decide where to draw another line. Use the compass to mark the same point on each wedge; then draw a line from that point to another point which may be anywhere inside the wedge. Check to see if you like the new shape you have created. Repeat the same line in each of the remaining wedges.

Drawing Curved Lines

Curved lines add interest to a quilt block. They are simple to draw with a compass, and if you are careful to draw gentle curves, they are easy to piece as well.

1. Draw a straight line and mark the center of it. Next draw the inner circle of the star. For the purposes of

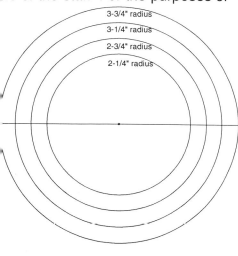

3-3/4" radius
3-1/4" radius
2-3/4" radius
2-1/4" radius

this exercise, draw a circle with a 2-1/4" radius. The complete circle will have a diameter of 4-1/2". Draw three more circles outside your first circle. The radius of each one should be 1/2" larger than the previous circle (2-3/4", 3-1/4", & 3-3/4"). The diameters of these same circles will measure 4-1/2, 5-1/2, 6-1/2, & 7-1/2. The outer circles provide guidelines, on which points can be easily marked to draw gentle curves.

2. Divide the circle into eight wedges. Draw additional lines, through all the circles, dividing each wedge in half. This will clearly identify the center of each wedge on the outer edge of the star.

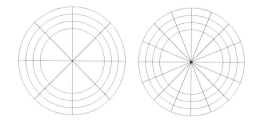

3. Place the point of the compass on the outer circle at the center of the wedge. Open the compass so the pencil point touches the intersection of the inner circle and the side of the wedge. Draw an arc which extends from one edge of the wedge to the other. Notice that the curve is very gradual.

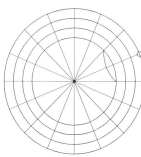

4. Draw the arc using the same point on the next smaller circle (6-1/2"). Notice that the curve is slightly deeper.

5. Now draw the arc using the center point on the circle which is next to the inner circle (5-1/2"). Notice the deepening curve. Use this arc for the remainder of this exercise. Draw the same arc in each wedge.

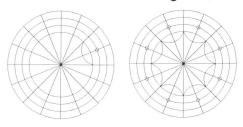

6. Draw another curved line inside the star. This time place the compass point on the intersection of the 4-1/2" circle and the arc. Extend the compass so the pencil point reaches the center of the wedge and touches the innermost part of the curve on the arc. Notice the gentleness of the curve. Draw this arc in each wedge.

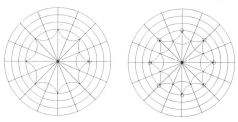

7. Now make some additional, straight lines inside the star to add interest to the center. First, place the compass on the center of the star and draw a circle with a 3/4" radius. Draw a triangle from the center of the innermost arc to the intersection of the small circle and the edge of the wedge. Draw a line to the same point on the other side of the wedge, and then back to the starting point. Repeat the same triangle in each wedge.

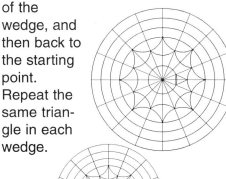

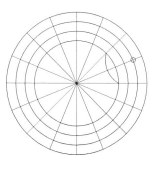

8. Erase the circles used as marking lines to draw the star.

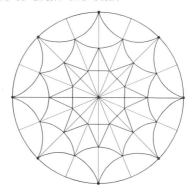

9. Erase the lines which divide each wedge in half. The star design is complete! See it's really not that difficult.

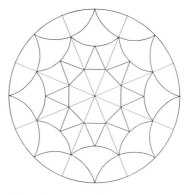

Tips For Successful Drawing and Piecing

1. Avoid drawing lots of lines that come together in a point. These make very narrow points that are nearly impossible to sew.

2. It's easy to draw something on paper that is impossible to sew. Avoid intersections with pesky pivot points where angles are something other than 90°.

3. Avoid drawing very tiny pieces that disappear into the design and are nearly impossible to sew. If you can't hold it easily in your fingers it's too small!

4. When creating curves, be careful to draw gentle curves that will not be too difficult to piece. Larger pieces are easier to handle. Avoid small, deep curves.

PIECING STARS

It really is no harder to stitch together a pie shaped wedge than a square block. The number of pieces vary, just like the average quilt block and difficulty ranges from very simple to somewhat involved. There are some general "rules" which, if followed, can make stitching stars simple and rewarding.

Templates

Templates are essential in making the unusual shapes created by star designs. Precision piecing relies on perfect cutting which requires perfect templates. It's really very simple to make templates.

1. For original designs trace each of the shapes, separately, from one wedge of the full size drawing of the star, onto another piece of paper. Use the most accurate wedge to make templates. Make all templates from the same wedge. For the patterns included in the book trace each shape from the full size wedge or template pattern.

2. Add 1/4" seam allowances to each side of these templates. To add the seam allowance to curved pieces use the compass. Open the compass points so they are 1/4" larger than the finished edges of the template. Draw this curved line.

3. My favorite way to make templates is somewhat unorthodox—actually I've never seen anyone else use this technique. However, it is simple and accurate. Begin with spray glue (I use 3-M Spray Mount™ Artist's Adhesive) and a manila file folder (or some other thin cardboard like the side of a cereal box, an insert from a shirt or stockings, etc). Spray the back side of the paper templates, and then stick them to the thin cardboard. The templates are ready to be cut out with a pair of paper scissors.

4. The templates in this book are designed to be cut with the template right side up on the right side of the fabric. However, many templates must be used both right side up and reversed. These are identified in the cutting directions as "Cut 6 plus 6(r) of piece B", with (r) indicating cutting from the reverse side of the template.

Grain

Wherever possible the grain line will follow the outside edge of the pie shaped wedge. Note the grain on the curved outer pieces is parallel to the outer edge. It helps to mark the grain line on the template.

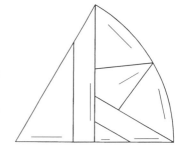

Cutting

There are several ways to approach this step. Use the technique you are most comfortable with. Probably the most standard method is to draw around the template with a sharp pencil and cut on this line with a pair of scissors. The time-saving technique I prefer is to cut around the templates with a rotary cutter. Use a ruler designed for use with a rotary cutter. Place the template on the fabric, with the drawn grain line matching the grain of the fabric. Then align the ruler with the cutting edge of the template, and cut the desired piece. Move the ruler to cut each side of the template. My favorite ruler for cutting individual templates is the 4" square ruler. Its small size enables you to easily turn it in any direction necessary for cutting.

Tips for Cutting

1. Look at the full size drawing and number each different template used in the star.

2. Count how many pieces to cut from each template. Do some need to be cut all in one direction? Do you need to cut some pieces in reverse?

3. If you have to cut several pieces from one template, cut a strip of fabric which is the measurement of the widest part of that template.

4. Lay all of the cut pieces on a 16" square ruler or a flannel board. Place the pieces in the same order as the master drawing. Look to make sure you have cut the necessary number of pieces and that you like the color arrangement.

The Perfect Quarter Inch

When is a quarter inch not a quarter inch? Actually, this is the usual case. Throughout my years of teaching I have seen quarter inches vary from 1/8" to nearly 1/2", sometimes all within the same block. To be successful stitching these blocks, it is essential that your seam allowance be exact.

Take the time necessary to perfect your 1/4" seam allowance. It will make future piecing projects accurate and much easier to sew. Cut three 1-1/2" x 6" pieces of fabric. Sew them together along the long edge and press. The width of the three sewn together should be 3-1/2". If it is greater than this your seam allowance is too small; smaller and your seam allowance is too big. Keep practicing until you achieve a perfect 1/4" seam allowance.

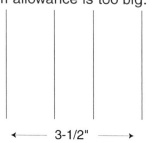

←——— 3-1/2" ———→

There are many specialized presser feet on the market today to make stitching a quarter inch seam a snap. One generic foot that fits most machines is manufactured by Little Foot, Ltd.®. The right edge of this foot is exactly 1/4" from the center needle position so all you need to do is use the edge of the foot as your guide. It's a good idea to test your 1/4" even when using a 1/4" presser foot.

Fixing a Less-Than-Perfect Quarter Inch

Circular star designs have several seams that join in the center of each block. This means that each inaccurate seam allowance magnifies problems in the center of the block, often creating a bonnet or ruffled edge rather than a flat block. Seam allowances that are greater than 1/4" cause the bonnet effect, while those less than 1/4" create ruffled edges. Generally the problem only becomes evident once you have stitched the final seam.

Sometimes, if the problem is relatively minor, it can be fixed with careful pressing. First set the circular star into the background square as explained on page 10. At this point the star can literally be blocked, just like blocking a sweater or blanket. Place a towel flat on an ironing board or other surface which can become wet. Pin the square so it measures the exact size it should be. Spray it with plain water until it is thoroughly wet. Cover the block with a clean lightweight piece of fabric and let the block dry. When dry, the block usually conforms to size. I always find this rather amazing, but it does work.

The bonnet effect is more common than ruffled edges. If this is a recurring problem, try slightly increasing the amount of seam allowance toward the center of the star as you stitch the wedges together. Begin

stitching at the outside of the wedge with a 1/4" seam allowance. As you work toward the center, gradually increase the seam allowance to about 5/16". Be careful to be consistent when stitching each wedge. The final seam may be somewhat larger than 1/4".

General Piecing Instructions

The stars in this book have been divided into either three, four, or five wedge circles, or multiples of those numbers. Wedges are assembled in the same fashion regardless of the number of wedges per star. Generally wedges are stitched together from the widest (outside) edge toward the center. Press seam allowances away from points, since this will reduce bulk and help make perfect points.

The wedges do not always stitch together in the most evident manner. I always place the pieces for each wedge right side up on my large 16" square ruler so I can easily determine what should be stitched together next.

Pick up two adjacent pieces, place right sides together and stitch. Often the angles of adjacent pieces will seem not to fit together. The way to determine if a piece is correctly aligned is to lay the pieces side by side with right sides up. The edges should form a straight line. If the edge is not perfectly straight and the edge makes an angle at the intersection of the two pieces, then you may have inadvertently turned one of the pieces.

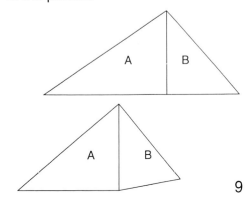

9

Once the pieces have been placed with right sides together, offset the points creating a "dog ear" effect forming a "V" in the center. The needle will fit exactly into the center of the "V" if the offset is correct and the seam allowance is a perfect 1/4".

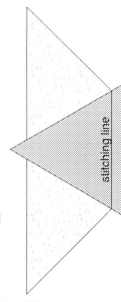

A slick trick to help with matching points is to use a 1/8" hole punch to make a hole in the template at each corner. Make a pencil dot through this hole onto the fabric and match these pencil points when sewing.

When a number of points adjoin, the easiest way to perfection is to place a pin though the exact points to be joined. Leave this pin sticking vertically through both pieces. Then place one pin on each side of this point barely catching all layers. I leave the vertical pin in place as I stitch carefully to that point and remove the pin just before I sew over it.

Refer to the piecing diagrams for each block and stitch as directed in the instructions. Be sure to press as directed.

Setting the Circular Star into the Background Square

1. Most of the blocks in this book are 12" finished. The background piece is the same for each of these blocks. The template for this background square is on page 14. Stitch four background pieces together to form a square with a circle cut out from the center. Fold this piece in half, matching seam line to seam line, then fold the narrow edges up to meet the center. Press these corners to identify the diagonal lines of the square without marking them.

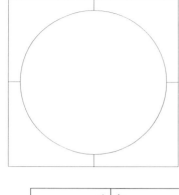

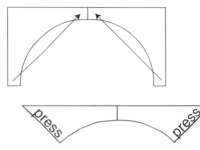

2. Repeat this procedure with the circular star. It will not be necessary to mark stars with eight wedges since their diagonal lines will already be identified by stitching lines. However, six-pointed and five-pointed stars do not have seams at the diagonals.

3. Pin the star to the background square, matching vertical, horizontal, and diagonal lines. The curves of the outer star edges are very gradual and should easily stretch or ease together. Pin two to three times between these points.

4. Stitch with the star on top and the background on bottom. This will enable you to see the points of the star while stitching and avoid cutting off points.

5. Once all of the star blocks are complete, find their average measurement, and trim or press, page 9, each block to a uniform size.

WINDOWPANE SASHING

Windowpane sashing is borders surrounding the individual blocks. It has several advantages. It allows you to create a wide variety of sizes from a single block size. For instance, a 12" block can become 13", 14" or even 16" using this method. It also allows for unequal sized blocks to become the same size by adding varying borders to create a uniform size. These blocks can then be set together in a number of different ways.

1. To make windowpane sashing, first determine the number and width of the borders to frame the quilt blocks. Remember that the outermost border will meet the outermost border of the block next to it - making it appear to be twice as wide.

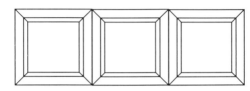

The illustration above is windowpane sashing with a 1" inner and a 2" outer border, making a finished block size of 18".

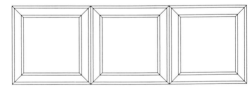

Sashing with 1/2" inner and outer and 1-1/2" center borders makes a finished block size of 17".

2. Cut strips on the crosswise grain of the fabric, being sure to add 1/2" for seam allowances. It will take about two strips (45" long) for each block. Therefore, if you plan a 1" inner and a 2" outer border, you will need to cut two strips that measure 1-1/2" x 45" and two strips that measure 2-1/2" x 45" for each block. Use the following chart to help determine yardage. If you are using more than twelve blocks combine the yardage

n the chart. For example, you have 16 blocks with 1" finished sashing. Add the yardage for four blocks, 3/8 yd., and twelve blocks, 1-1/8 yd., for a total of 1-1/2 yards.

# Blocks /	# Strips /	Yardage
1/2" sashing, strips 1" x 45"		
4	8	1/4 yd.
9	18	5/8 yd.
12	24	3/4 yd.
1" sashing, strips 1-1/2" x 45"		
4	8	3/8 yd.
9	18	7/8 yd.
12	24	1-1/8 yds.
1-1/2" sashing, strips 2" x 45"		
4	8	1/2 yd.
9	18	1-1/8 yds.
12	24	1-1/2 yds.
2" sashing, strips 2-1/2" x 45"		
4	8	5/8 yd.
9	18	1-3/8 yds.
12	24	1-7/8 yds.

3. Stitch sashing strips together along the long edge to make strip sets. Press seams in alternating directions. This means that the strips used on the sides of a block will have seams pressed toward the outside edge of the the border, while the seams of the top and bottom borders will be pressed toward the inside edge of the border.

4. Cut the strip sets to the required length. To calculate this measurement add together the width of the block, twice the width of the sashing, plus an extra 2".

Example: For a 12" block with a 1" and 2" windowpane, cut the strip set 20" or 12" + 2(1"+2") + 2".

5. Center and stitch the top and bottom windowpane to the quilt block, starting and stopping 1/4" from the edge of the block. Backstitch at each end. Repeat with the sides.

6. Miter the corners of the block. Fold the block in half on the diagonal. Use a ruler with a 45° angle to mark the stitching lines. Pin carefully, making certain the outer edges match. Stitch.

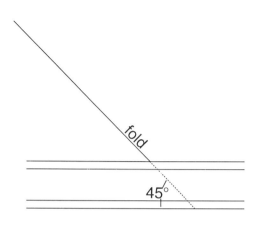

Trim seam allowances to 1/4" and press toward one side. Generally, the seams will press more easily in one direction. Press toward the side of least resistance.

7. Measure all of the blocks and trim to an average size, using a 16" square rotary ruler. If the blocks should measure 15-1/2", you will probably find that some measure only 15" while others measure as much as 15-3/4". Trim the blocks to an average size, in this case 15-3/8". Trim an equal amount from each side of the block. Trimming from just two sides will result in chopped off corners. Those blocks that are smaller than average can be gently stretched to fit when the blocks are sewn together.

DESIGN A SETTING

There are a variety of innovative ways to sew the windowpaned blocks together. Planning your own setting results in a larger quilt and an original design. It's relatively easy to plan the arrangement using graph paper. For this step it doesn't matter if the graph paper is perfectly accurate. You will be making a scale drawing of your quilt. I generally use 11" x 17" graph paper with four squares per inch.

Look at books and magazines to gather ideas for ways to set the blocks together. A book I highly recommend is "Blockbuster Quilts" by Margaret Miller.

1. Decide on the scale for the drawing. This should be a number that easily divides into the finished size of your quilt blocks. For instance, if the finished block is 12", you may choose the scale of 2" = 1 square (1/4"); a 15" finished block may have a scale of 3" = 1 square (1/4"), etc.

2. Draw the placement of blocks on graph paper. Notice that this arrangement leaves a large empty space in the middle of the quilt.

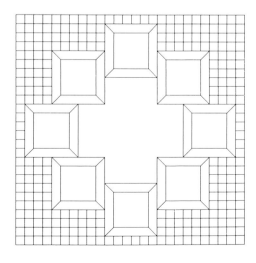

You may choose to fill this space with a custom designed star or you may elect to add another bordered block. Notice how the addition of another block fills the space, leaving an empty rectangle on each side.

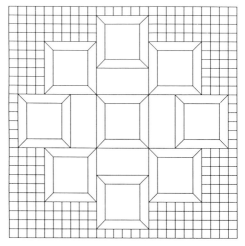

3. Think about ways to fill in this space. Draw a simple geometric shape in the rectangle.

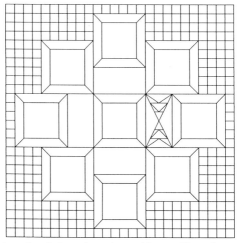

Look at the drawing. If you like the way it looks, repeat the drawing on all four sides. This will become the inner border.

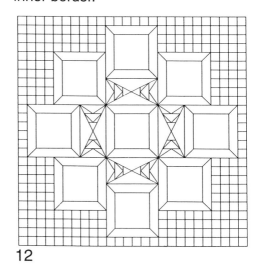

4. Using the scale drawing, make a full-size drawing of this design. It's easy! If each square equals 2", then draw a line 2" long for each square in the drawing. Mark the full size drawing with lines that correspond to those on the graph paper. You may need to draw a full-size grid that corresponds to the graph paper grid.

5. Make templates for the borders, adding 1/4" seam allowance, as described on page 8. Cut out a small portion of the setting, possibly only enough pieces to surround one block. Place these pieces around the star block. Step back and view the arrangement. Do you like the design? Is there contrast between the block and the setting? If you are pleased with the arrangement, then cut out enough pieces to complete the setting.

6. There may be several areas of the quilt which contain only plain pieces of background fabric. Use the grid (remember the scale of your drawing) to determine what size to cut these pieces. Remember to add a 1/4" seam allowance to each side.

7. Stitch the blocks together, following the plan in the scale drawing. Generally you can sew the blocks into rows, then sew the rows together.

8. Add a narrow border around each side to make the quilt larger, and to offset the outer border from the blocks.

9. Repeat the inner border on the outside of the quilt. Notice that you may need to alter the border to make it fit the space.

TIP - The setting you choose for your blocks should be a display case for them. Keep the setting reasonably simple so it doesn't overpower the blocks.

TIP - I always finish one portion of a quilt top before making final decisions about what comes next. I sew all my blocks together before worrying about how to set them together. Then I work on the setting before worrying about the borders. I do this so I can view the quilt top each step of the way before committing to a setting or border which may look fine on paper, but may not work well color-wise or lacks contrast when actually used with the star blocks.

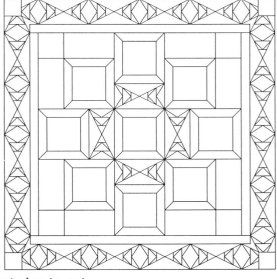

This is also the reason why I like to have many fabric choices when making a quilt and a lot of extra yardage. The key to success is choice!

FINISHING

The top is done, it's time to celebrate! But wait, the fun isn't over yet. There is an old saying which says, "It's not finished until it's quilted." Now is the time to think about the final process toward completion of your star quilt. There are many fine books with detailed instructions for both machine and hand quilting. I recommend "Heirloom Machine Quilting," by Harriet Hargrave along with a new book, "Machine Quilting Made Easy," by Maurine Noble. Harriet's book is a thorough, basic primer on this technique and includes several pages of continuous design quilting patterns to fit both blocks and borders. Maurine's book includes basic techniques and a wonderful introduction to machine embroidery and the use of decorative threads. "Easy Traditional Quilting", by Lora Rocke, available from Animas Quilts Publishing, is full of traditional quilting patterns adapted to continuous quilting lines.

1. The first decision is whether to hand or machine quilt. This influences the type of batting to purchase. Generally, machine quilting is most successful with cotton batting while polyester battings are used in hand-quilted projects.

2. Mark the quilting design on the quilt top. I recently discovered a new purpose for 3-M Spray Mount™ Artist's Adhesive. Photocopy the quilting designs. Then spray the back of the paper containing the design and stick it to the quilt top. Machine quilt the design right through the paper. Tear away the paper pattern, pulling slightly on the surface of the quilt to pull it away from the paper. Because this adhesive spray provides a re-stickable glue it does not permanently adhere to the surface of the quilt. It also leaves no sticky residue. *Caution: Don't apply the paper until you are ready to stitch.*

3. Piece the backing if necessary. The diagram next to the backing yardage with each quilt shows how the backing was pieced using the yardage given. You may wish to use up scraps and do a little back art.

4. Layer the quilt. Either tape or clamp the backing fabric, wrong side up, to a large surface. A tile floor or two work tables pushed together work well. Pull the backing fabric so it is very flat, with no bubbles or wrinkles. It should also be straight.

Lay the batting on top of the backing. Pat it in place, working from the center outward to the edges. Sometimes, creases in the batting can be removed by placing the batting in the dryer on a fluff setting. Always read the directions on the batting package before use. Do not pin the batting in place or attach it in any way to the backing.

Place the quilt top, right side up, on top of the batting and backing. Baste, using safety pins for machine quilted projects and thread for hand quilted projects. Place the safety pins so you won't be quilting over them. Work from the center out when hand basting. First, baste vertically down the center of the quilt. Repeat at the horizontal center of the quilt. Then baste diagonally from corner to corner. Finally, baste a grid, both horizontal and vertical.

5. Quilt as desired.

6. Bind the quilt. Measure the perimeter of the quilt. This measurement equals the length of both sides plus the width of the top and bottom of the quilt. Cut enough binding strips to go completely around the quilt. I prefer to make a double binding because it is more durable and easier to work with than a single layer of fabric. Cut 2-1/2" wide binding strips either on the bias or crosswise grain of the fabric. Stitch the strips together end to end with right sides together. If the strips were cut on the crosswise grain, stitch together at right angles and then trim the excess fabric. Press seams open.

Press the binding strips in half, lengthwise, wrong sides together. Attach to the quilt with raw edges together and the binding on top. Leave 1" extra binding at each end. Stitch through all three layers with a 1/4" seam allowance, starting and stopping at the 1/4" seam line.

Miter the corners using a Binding Miter Tool© or your favorite method.

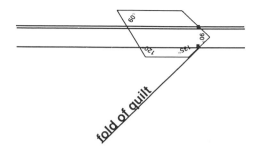

Turn the finished edge of the binding to the back, enclosing the raw edges of the quilt. Stitch in place by hand.

7. If the quilt is intended to hang on the wall, make a sleeve for hanging. A sleeve is a strip of fabric that is 8-1/2" wide and the width of the quilt. Stitch this strip into a long tube and hem each end. Whipstitch the sleeve in place along the top of the back of the quilt. Insert a dowel or curtain rod through the sleeve to hang the finished quilt.

8. Sign your quilt. We have no way of knowing which of our quilts may last a hundred years. Quilt historians today lament the fact that the makers of many exquisite quilts will remain forever unknown merely because they did not have the foresight to place their name or some other identification on their masterpiece. We've also all heard the stories of Aunt Mildred's quilt collection which was passed down to her by a maternal aunt or other unknown relative. Don't let this be the fate of your quilt. Be proud of it and take the time to place your name somewhere on the quilt, either front or back. Do you have a star that didn't turn out quite as well as you would have liked? Sign it and stitch it to the back.

GEᴎEᴙᴀʟ ᴊᴎꙄᴛᴙᴜᴄᴛᴊᴏᴎꙄ ᖴᴏᴙ ʙʟᴏᴄᴋꙄ ᴀᴎᴅ ᴏᴜᴊʟᴛꙄ

12" Star Blocks

There are patterns for twelve Blocks of the Month, plus variations. All of these blocks are 12" finished. In addition there are three 12" blocks in this section which were designed by students while making their quilts. Each block is referenced to at least one photograph.

When making a block, first decide which variation to use. This will determine how to cut the templates and the number needed of each. A block with eight wedges may need eight of each template or four plus four reversed.

Each block has a drawing of the star, and variations, and a full size wedge. Make the templates from the full size wedge. Be sure to add seam allowances. Directions for making templates are on page 8.

All of the 12" blocks use the same template for the background square, as provided here. Directions for sewing the pieced star to it are on page 10.

Quilt Directions

Most of the quilts included here use 12" blocks. When the directions instruct you to make Star Blocks, choose from this section or draft your own.

Some of the quilts use star blocks that finish other than 12". Complete instructions for these are with the quilt directions. Again, full size wedges are given. Make the templates from these, being sure to add seam allowances.

Cutting instructions are given at the beginning of each project. You may cut everything at once or cut as you go. If you cut all the pieces at once, be sure to label them. The advantage to cutting as you go allows you to make minor adjustments in measurements. If your measurements are consistently different, check your seam allowance. When cutting as you go, you will be cutting star pieces first. Be sure to leave enough fabric for sashing, borders, etc. when necessary.

Measurements are given as sections of the quilt are completed. For ease in measuring these include the seam allowance. For example you may be directed to make eight 12-1/2" Star Blocks. When you measure and block or trim them they need to measure 12-1/2". The directions may state that after adding windowpanes the blocks measure 16-1/2". This means the block should measure 16-1/2" unfinished, it will be 16" once it is sewn into the quilt.

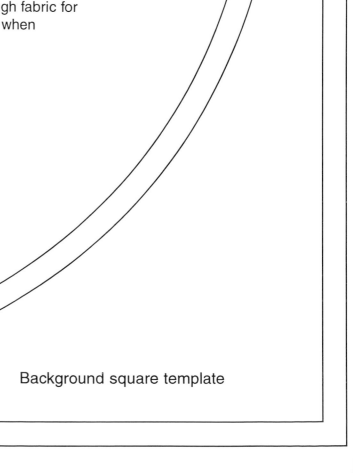

Background square template

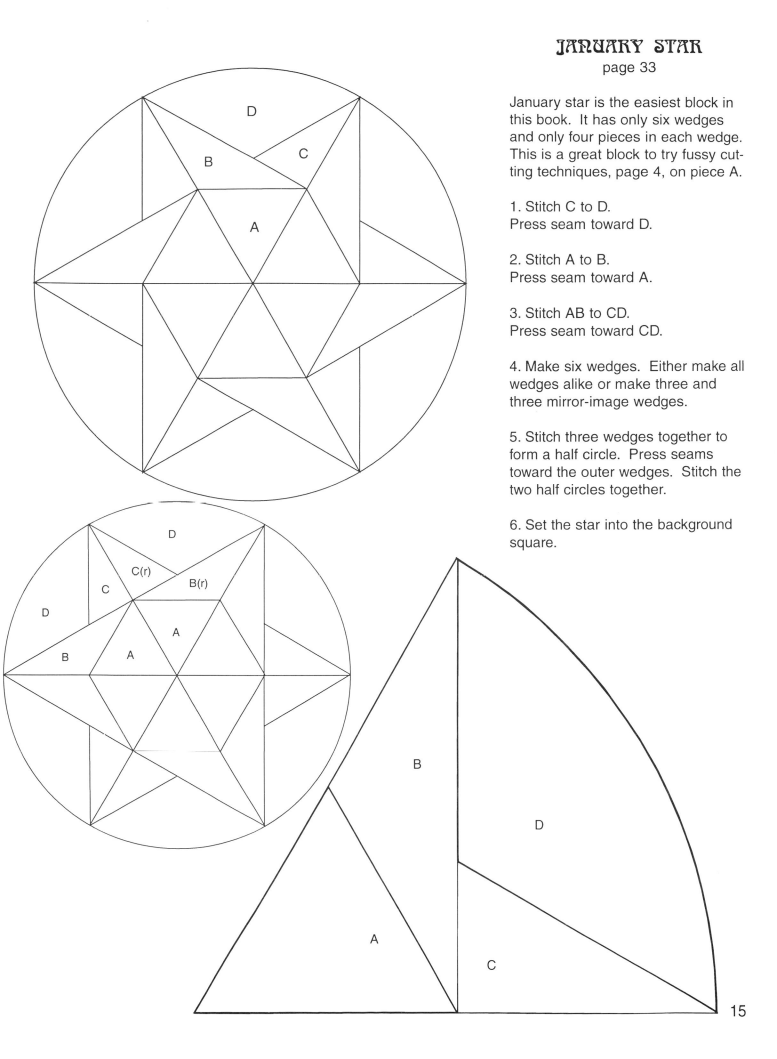

January star is the easiest block in this book. It has only six wedges and only four pieces in each wedge. This is a great block to try fussy cutting techniques, page 4, on piece A.

1. Stitch C to D.
Press seam toward D.

2. Stitch A to B.
Press seam toward A.

3. Stitch AB to CD.
Press seam toward CD.

4. Make six wedges. Either make all wedges alike or make three and three mirror-image wedges.

5. Stitch three wedges together to form a half circle. Press seams toward the outer wedges. Stitch the two half circles together.

6. Set the star into the background square.

15

FEBRUARY STAR

pages 40 and 37

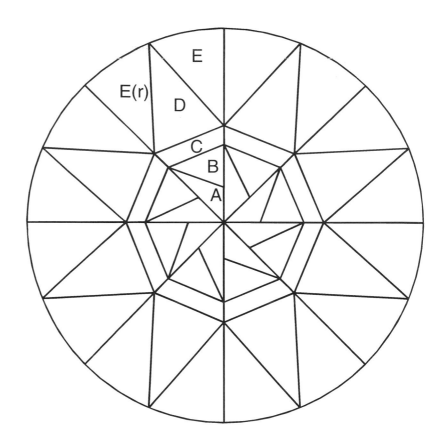

This month's star has eight wedges. It is easy to check for accuracy in an eight-pointed circle. Two wedges=1/4 circle. After you've stitched the first two wedges together measure to see if the inside forms a square (90°) corner.

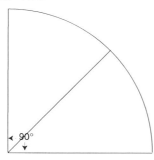

90°

1. Stitch A to B. Press seam toward A.

2. Stitch E to D. Press seam toward E. Stitch E(r) to DE. Press seam toward E(r).

3. Stitch C to AB. Press seam toward C.

4. Stitch ABC to DE. Press seam toward C.

5. Make eight wedges. Either make all the wedges alike or make four and four mirror-image wedges.

6. Stitch the wedges into pairs. Press seams in one consistent direction, because this causes less bulk in the center of the star. Check to see if the inside corners form a square corner.

Stitch the pairs together to form half circles. Stitch the half circles together.

7. Set the star into the background square.

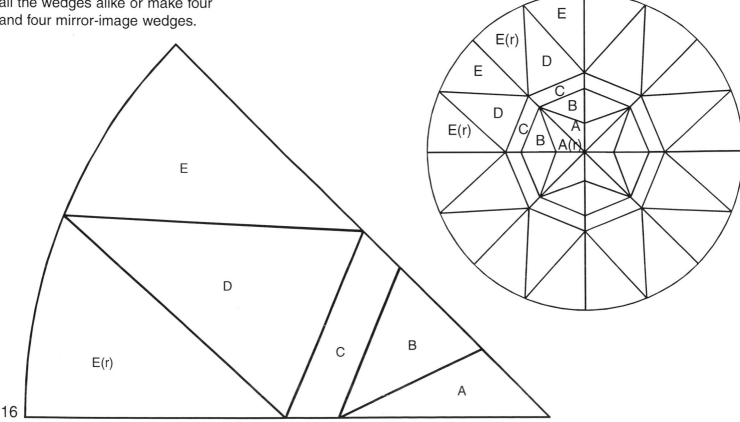

March star resembles a pinwheel, reminiscent of the March winds. However, if you make this design with every other wedge a mirror-image it looks completely different.

1. Stitch A to B.
Press seam toward A.

2. Stitch C to AB.
Press seam toward C.

3. Stitch D to E.
Press seam toward E.

4. Stitch ABC to DE.
Press seam toward DE.

5. Make eight wedges. Either make all the wedges alike or make four mirror-image wedges.

6. Stitch wedges together into pairs. Press these seams consistently in one direction to reduce bulk at the center of the star. Stitch wedges together to form half circles. Stitch the half circles together.

7. Set the star into the background square.

17

APRIL STAR

page 40

April star is one of my favorites. It lends itself well to a narrow stripe or a bold accent fabric bordering the inner star. Even though it has seven pieces per wedge, the total number of pieces per star is only 42.

1. Stitch E to F. Press seam toward F. Stitch EF to F(r). Press seam toward F(r).

2. Stitch C to D. Press seam toward C.

3. Stitch CD to EF. Press seam toward EF.

4. Stitch A to B. Press seam toward B.

5. Stitch AB to CDEF. Press seam toward CDEF.

6. Make six wedges. Either make all the wedges alike or make three and three mirror-image wedges.

7. Stitch three wedges together to form half circles. Press seams toward the outer wedges. Stitch the half circles together.

8. Set the star into the background square.

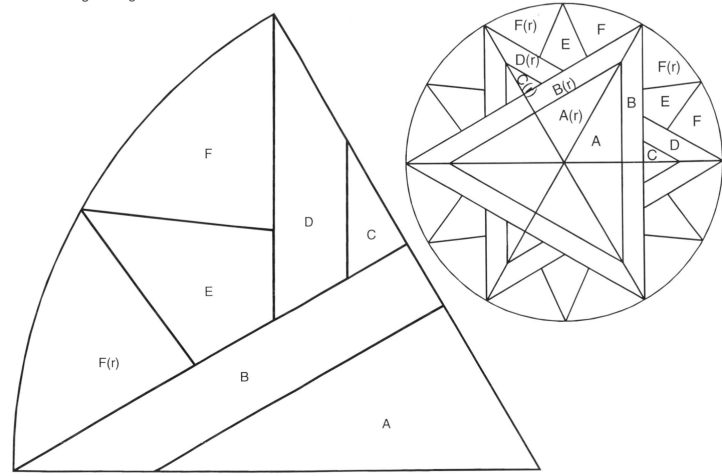

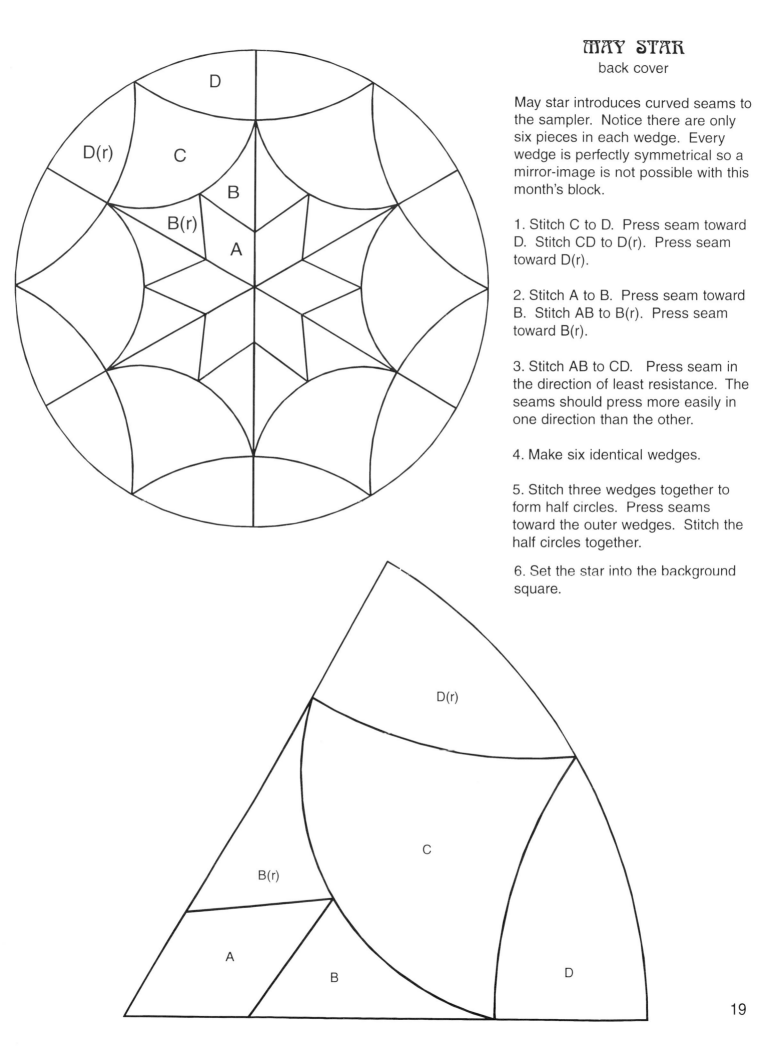

MAY STAR
back cover

May star introduces curved seams to the sampler. Notice there are only six pieces in each wedge. Every wedge is perfectly symmetrical so a mirror-image is not possible with this month's block.

1. Stitch C to D. Press seam toward D. Stitch CD to D(r). Press seam toward D(r).

2. Stitch A to B. Press seam toward B. Stitch AB to B(r). Press seam toward B(r).

3. Stitch AB to CD. Press seam in the direction of least resistance. The seams should press more easily in one direction than the other.

4. Make six identical wedges.

5. Stitch three wedges together to form half circles. Press seams toward the outer wedges. Stitch the half circles together.

6. Set the star into the background square.

19

JUNE STAR

pages 36 and 40

Swirling curves with a narrow border combine the effects of April and May, essentially a twist of both. The June star also looks terrific with half of the wedges made in mirror-image.

1. Stitch D to E.
Press seam toward E.

2. Stitch B to C.
Press seam toward C.

3. Stitch A to BC.
Press seam toward BC.

4. Stitch ABC to DE.
Press seam toward DE.

5. Make eight wedges. Either make all wedges alike or make four and four mirror-image wedges.

6. Stitch wedges together into pairs. Press these seams consistently in one direction to reduce bulk in the center of the star. Stitch the quarter circles together to form half circles. Press seams in the same direction as the other seams. Stitch the half circles together.

7. Set the star into the background square.

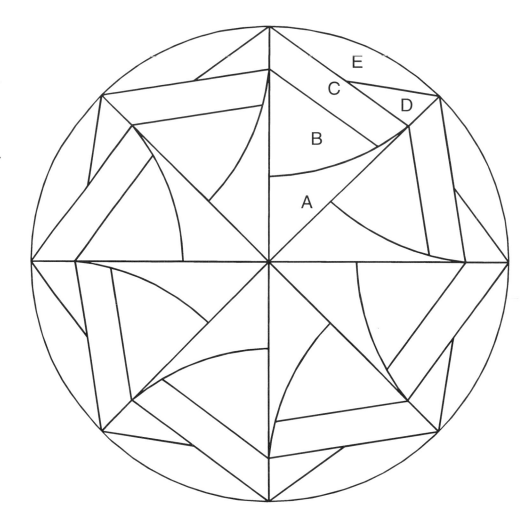

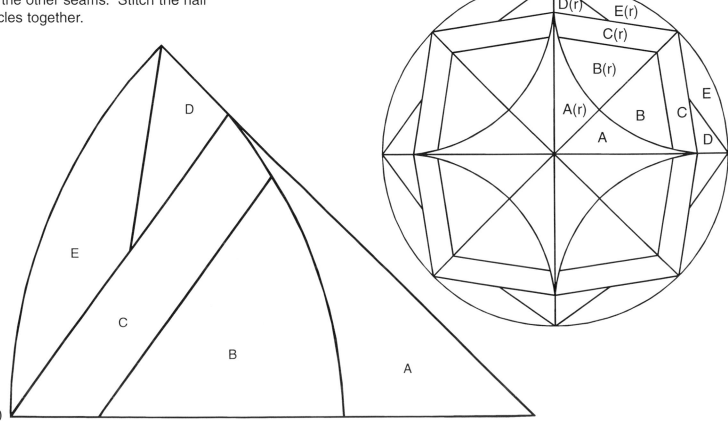

20

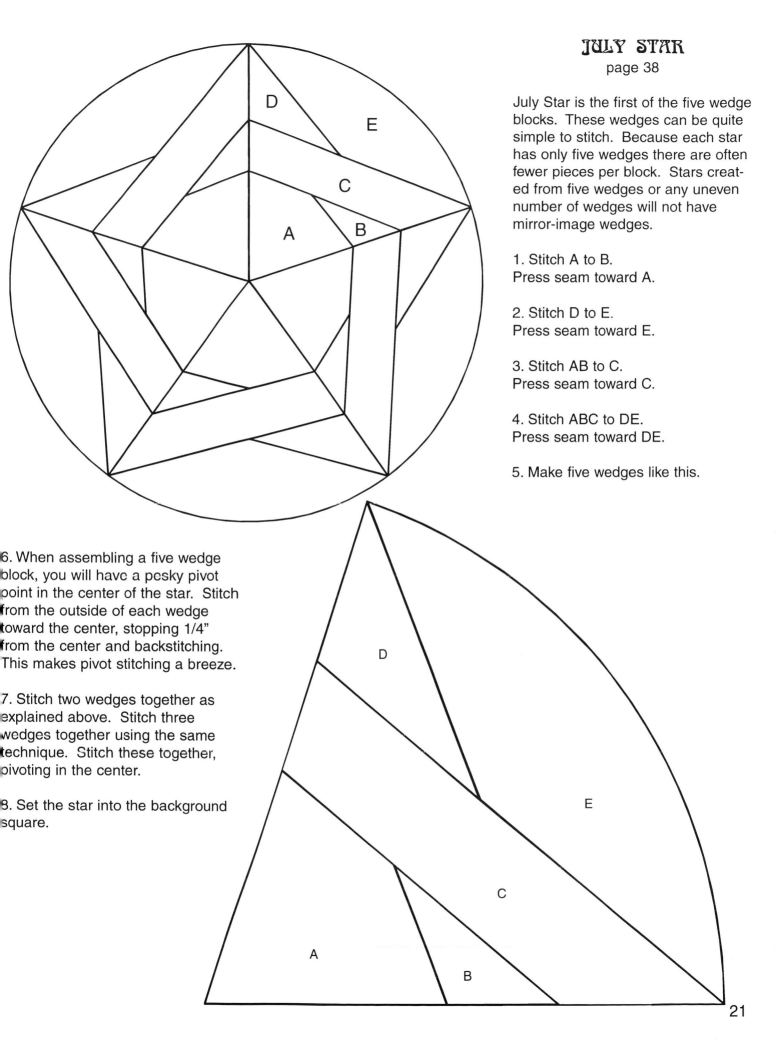

July Star is the first of the five wedge blocks. These wedges can be quite simple to stitch. Because each star has only five wedges there are often fewer pieces per block. Stars created from five wedges or any uneven number of wedges will not have mirror-image wedges.

1. Stitch A to B.
Press seam toward A.

2. Stitch D to E.
Press seam toward E.

3. Stitch AB to C.
Press seam toward C.

4. Stitch ABC to DE.
Press seam toward DE.

5. Make five wedges like this.

6. When assembling a five wedge block, you will have a pesky pivot point in the center of the star. Stitch from the outside of each wedge toward the center, stopping 1/4" from the center and backstitching. This makes pivot stitching a breeze.

7. Stitch two wedges together as explained above. Stitch three wedges together using the same technique. Stitch these together, pivoting in the center.

8. Set the star into the background square.

AUGUST STAR

page 36

No tricks in August Star, except one additional pesky pivot point. This time it's in the middle of each wedge as well as in the center of the star.

1. Stitch D to E and D(r) to E(r). Press seam toward E. Stitch these two units together, stitching from the outside edge of the wedge inward, stopping and backstitching 1/4" from the inside edge.

2. Stitch B to C, stopping and back-stitching 1/4" from the edge at the narrowest point of B. Press seam toward C. Stitch C(r) to the other side, again stopping 1/4" from the edge. Press seam toward C(r).

3. Stitch A to BC. Press seam toward A.

4. Stitch ABC to DE, pivoting at the center.

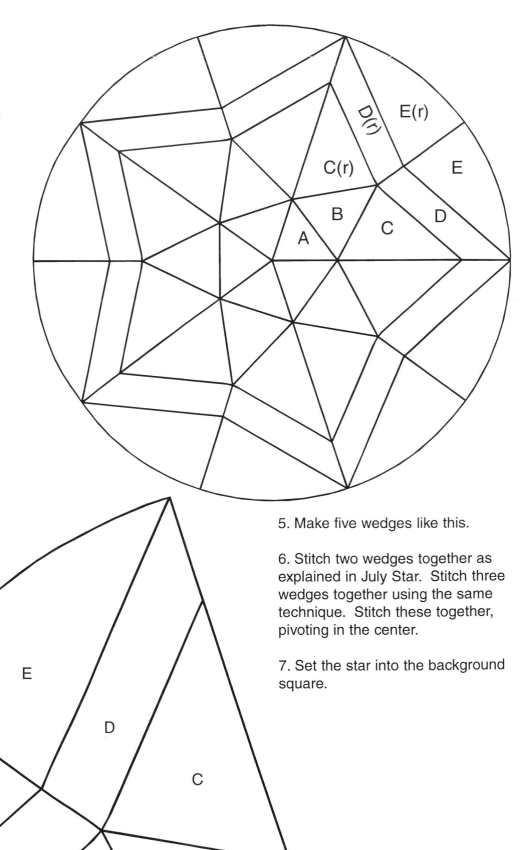

5. Make five wedges like this.

6. Stitch two wedges together as explained in July Star. Stitch three wedges together using the same technique. Stitch these together, pivoting in the center.

7. Set the star into the background square.

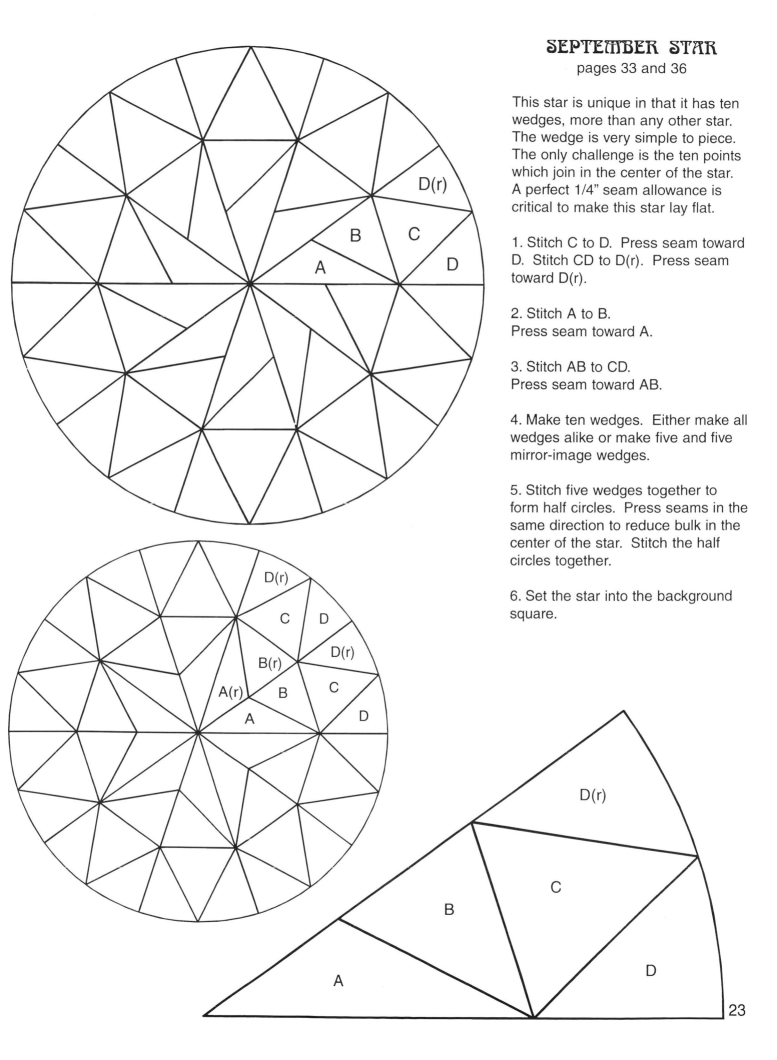

SEPTEMBER STAR

pages 33 and 36

This star is unique in that it has ten wedges, more than any other star. The wedge is very simple to piece. The only challenge is the ten points which join in the center of the star. A perfect 1/4" seam allowance is critical to make this star lay flat.

1. Stitch C to D. Press seam toward D. Stitch CD to D(r). Press seam toward D(r).

2. Stitch A to B. Press seam toward A.

3. Stitch AB to CD. Press seam toward AB.

4. Make ten wedges. Either make all wedges alike or make five and five mirror-image wedges.

5. Stitch five wedges together to form half circles. Press seams in the same direction to reduce bulk in the center of the star. Stitch the half circles together.

6. Set the star into the background square.

23

OCTOBER STAR
front cover and page 36

October star was designed by Helen Duncan. This star is made from two different wedges which are referred to as A and B. Because of the two-wedge design it is possible to create at least five different designs with these two wedges. The basic designs are shown here to allow you to choose the combination you wish. Best of all, it is deceptively easy to sew!

Wedge A

1. Stitch C to D.
Press seam toward D.

2. Stitch E to F.
Press seam toward E.

3. Stitch EF to A.
Press seam toward EF.

4. Stitch EFA to CD.
Press seam toward CD.

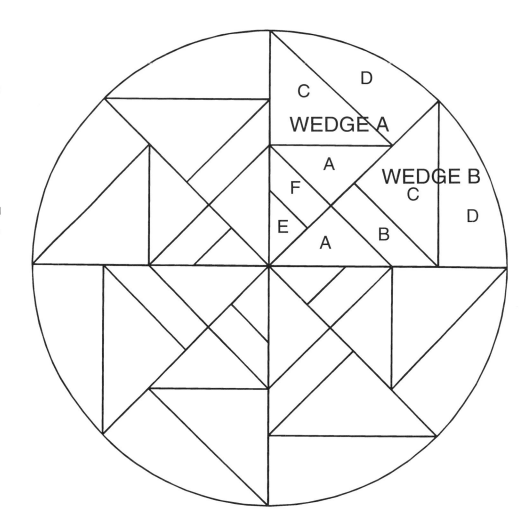

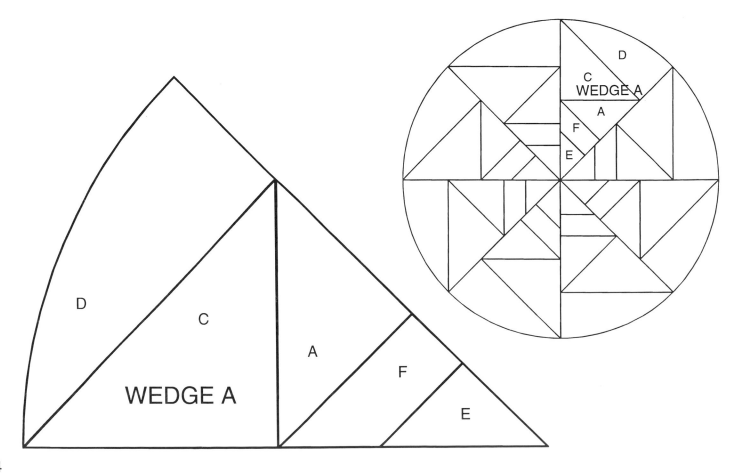

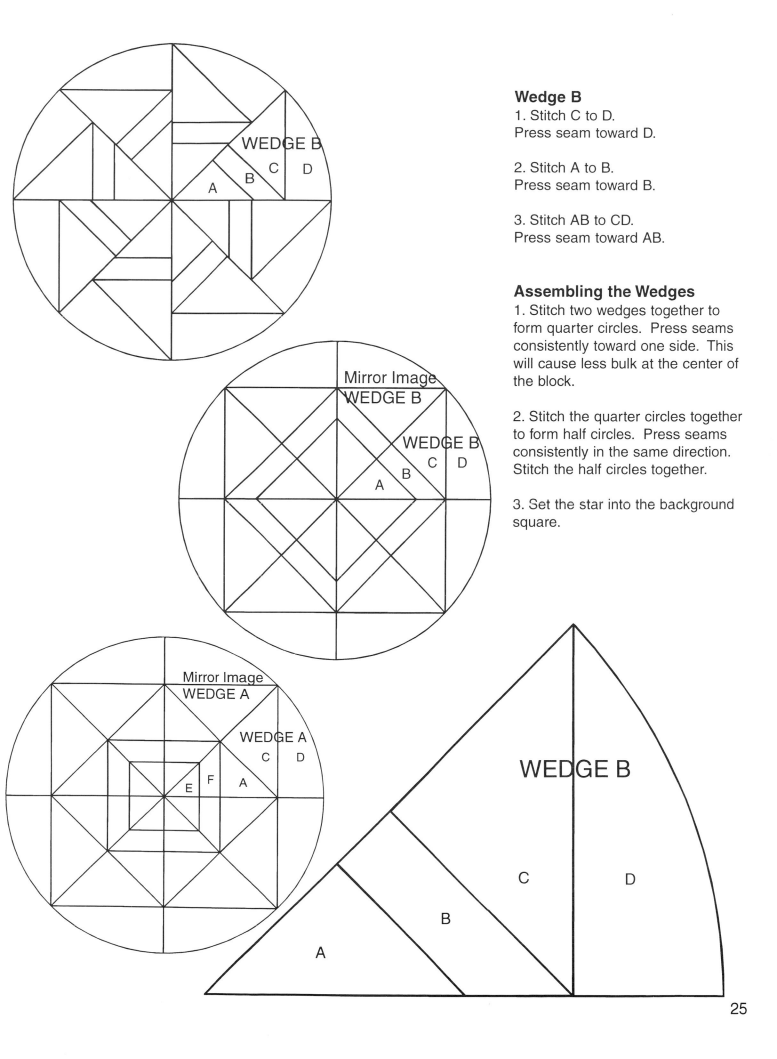

Wedge B

1. Stitch C to D.
Press seam toward D.

2. Stitch A to B.
Press seam toward B.

3. Stitch AB to CD.
Press seam toward AB.

Assembling the Wedges

1. Stitch two wedges together to form quarter circles. Press seams consistently toward one side. This will cause less bulk at the center of the block.

2. Stitch the quarter circles together to form half circles. Press seams consistently in the same direction. Stitch the half circles together.

3. Set the star into the background square.

WEDGE B

WEDGE B

Mirror Image
WEDGE B

WEDGE B

Mirror Image
WEDGE A

WEDGE A

WEDGE B

NOVEMBER STAR

page 36

November star was designed by Anita McSorley. This star may be a challenge to stitch with 60 pieces in the star alone. There are no mirror-image wedges.

1. Stitch G to F. Press seam toward F. Stitch F(r) to the other side of G. Press seam toward F(r).

2. Stitch D(r) to H. Press seam toward H.

3. Stitch DH to FGF. Press seam toward DH.

4. Stitch A to B. Press seam toward A.

5. Stitch C to D. Press seam toward D.

6. Stitch AB to CD. Press seam toward CD.

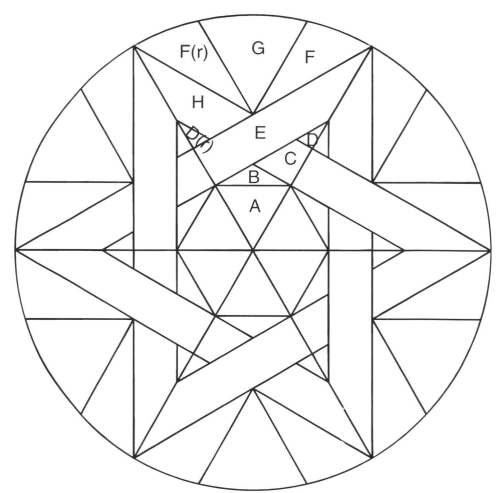

7. Stitch ABCD to E. Press seam toward E.

8. Stitch ABCDE to FGH. Press seam toward FGH.

9. Make six wedges like this.

10. Stitch three wedges together to form half circles. Press seams toward the outer wedges. Stitch the half circles together.

11. Set the star into the background square.

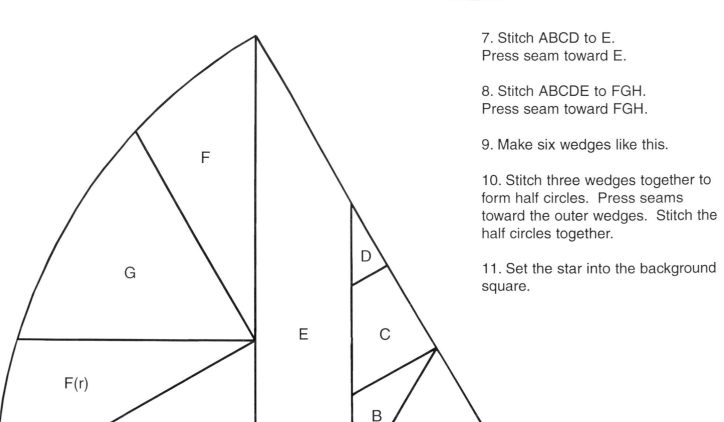

26

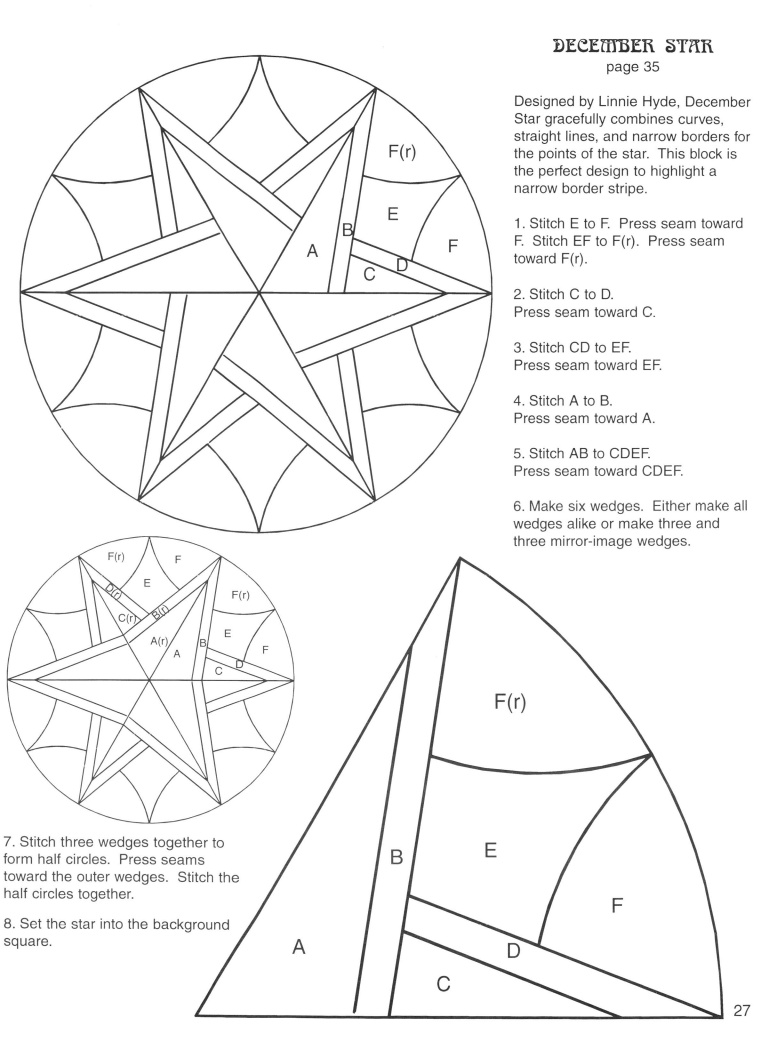

Designed by Linnie Hyde, December Star gracefully combines curves, straight lines, and narrow borders for the points of the star. This block is the perfect design to highlight a narrow border stripe.

1. Stitch E to F. Press seam toward F. Stitch EF to F(r). Press seam toward F(r).

2. Stitch C to D. Press seam toward C.

3. Stitch CD to EF. Press seam toward EF.

4. Stitch A to B. Press seam toward A.

5. Stitch AB to CDEF. Press seam toward CDEF.

6. Make six wedges. Either make all wedges alike or make three and three mirror-image wedges.

7. Stitch three wedges together to form half circles. Press seams toward the outer wedges. Stitch the half circles together.

8. Set the star into the background square.

STAR LIGHT

page 35

This block was designed by Linnie Hyde for the quilt Oh My Stars!

1. Stitch D to C. Press seam toward D. Stitch E to CD. Press seam toward E.

2. Stitch B to CDE. Press seam toward CDE.

3. Stitch A to BCDE. Press seam away from A.

4. Make eight wedges or make four, and four mirror-image wedges.

5. Stitch wedges together into quarter circles. Stitch these together into half circles. Stitch the half circles together.

6. Set the circular star into the background square.

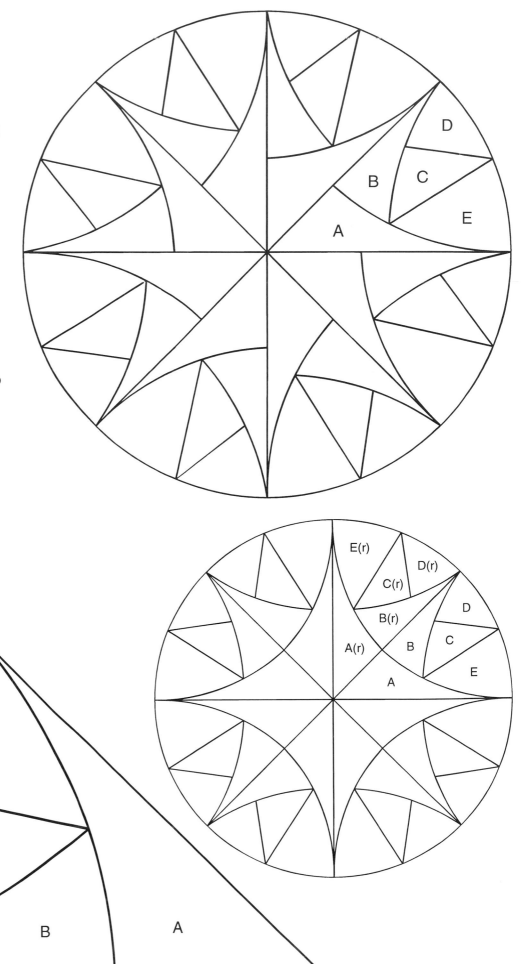

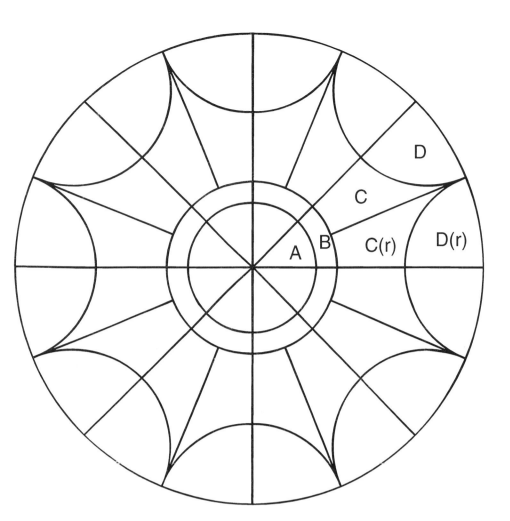

This block was designed by Linnie Hyde and is used in her quilt Oh My Stars!

1. Stitch A to B.
Press seam toward B.

2. Stitch C to D and C(r) to D(r).
Press seams toward D.

3. Stitch CD to C(r)D(r).
Press seam toward D(r).

4. Stitch AB to CD.
Make eight wedges.

5. Stitch two wedges together to form a quarter circle. Stitch these together to form a half circle. Stitch the half circles together.

6. Set the circular star into the background square.

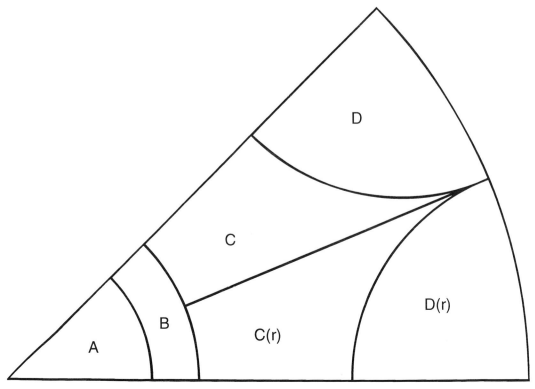

29

STAR IN A SQUARE

page 38

Designed by Sharon Johnson for her
quilt, A View From Sandi's Window.

1. Stitch E to F.
Press seam toward F.

2. Stitch D to EF.
Press seam toward EF.

3. Stitch A to B to C.
Press seam away from B.

4. Stitch ABC to DEF to complete
the wedge. Press seam toward C.
Make four wedges like this plus four
mirror-image wedges.

5. Stitch together two wedges (a regular and a mirror-image wedge) to
form quarter circles. Stitch these
together to form half circles. Stitch
the half circles together.

6. Set the star into a background
square.

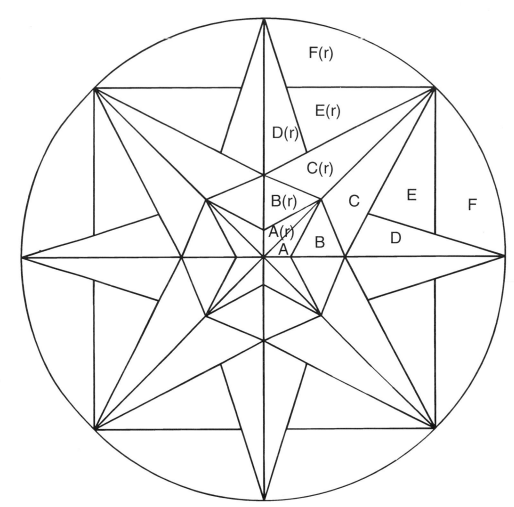

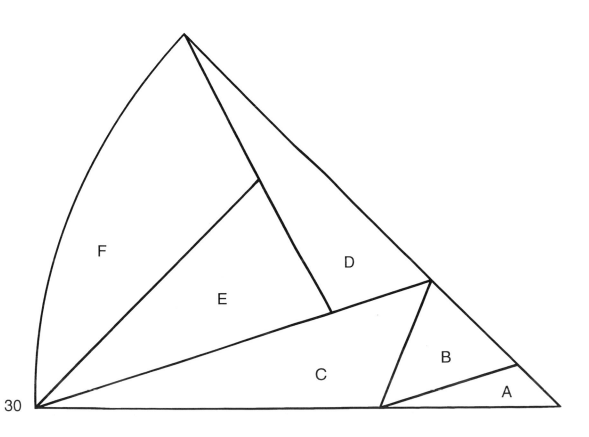

GECKO-MANIA

By Harriet Smith
38" x 38"
Page 39

This wall quilt was inspired by one piece of fabric, a wonderful gecko print in shades of purple and green. The gecko design is repeated in the border with geckos quilted using metallic thread.

YARDAGE

1/4 yd. Dark (star)
1/4 yd. Light (star background)
1/3 yd. Feature print (gecko)
1/3 yd. Triangle accent
1/4 yd. Inner border
5/8 yd. Medium (star & outer border)
5/8 yd. Accent (circle & binding)
1 yd. Background print (black)
1-1/4 yds. Backing

CUTTING

Dark
  Template B - cut 5
Light
  Template D - cut 5 plus 5(r)
Feature Print
  Template C - cut 5
  Four 3-1/2" squares
Triangle accent
  Template G - cut 30
Medium
  Four 3-1/2" strips for outer border
  Template A - cut 5
Accent
  Template E - cut 5
Background
  Cut one 30-1/2" square
  Template F - cut 30
  Template H - cut 30
Inner border
  Four 1-1/2" strips

Take this wedge to a photo copier to enlarge it 171%. The length of the straight sides will then be 12".

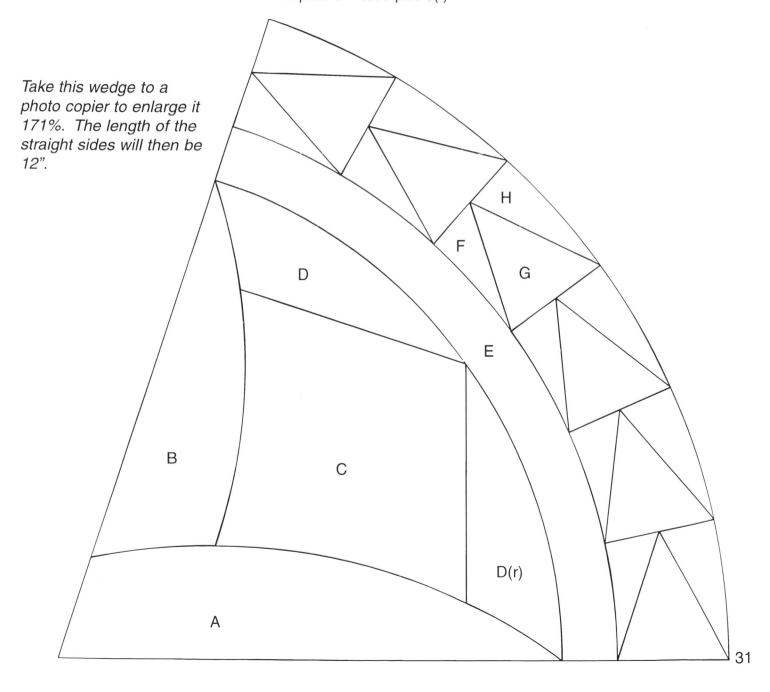

PIECING

1. Stitch D to C. Press seam toward D. Stitch D(r) to the opposite side of C. Press seam toward D(r).

2. Stitch B to CD. Press seam toward CD.

3. Stitch A to BCD. Press seam toward BCD.

4. Stitch ABCD to E. Press seam toward E.

5. Stitch F to G. Press seam toward F. Stitch H to the opposite side of G. Press seam toward H. Stitch six of these units together to form 1/5 of a circle. Stitch this unit to ABCDE.

6. Make five wedges like this.

7. Stitch four wedges together into pairs. Stitch the remaining wedge to one of the pairs, stopping 1/4" from the inner edge. Stitch the two wedge unit to the three wedge unit to complete the star.

8. Fold the 30-1/2" background square into quarters. Now fold it in half diagonally. Press lightly on the folds. Repeat with the star. Find the average measurement of the radius of the star. Use the compass to draw a circle with a radius 1/2" less in the center of the square. Cut out this circle. Place the star on the square, matching fold lines. Pin and sew as explained on page 10.

9. Attach the 1-1/2" inner border as you would a single border of windowpane sashing.

10. Measure and cut the 3-1/2" outer borders. Stitch a 3-1/2" outer border to both sides of the center square.

11. Stitch the 3-1/2" squares to each end of the remaining two border strips. Stitch these borders to the top and bottom of the quilt top.

12. Refer to finishing, page 12, for ideas on how to complete your project.

Peek-A-Boo Stars
Janet Wolfe, Albuquerque, New Mexico
78" x 79"

Stars In My Garden
Darlene Jones, Tijeras, New Mexico
105" x 96"

Oh My Stars!
Linnie Hyde, Albuquerque, New Mexico
90" x 90"

36

Above: **Star Studded Compass**
Janet Wolfe, Albuquerque, New Mexico
80" x 88"

Left: **Circus of the Stars**
Gail Garber, Rio Rancho, New Mexico
62" x 80"

A View From Sandi's Window
Sharon Johnson, Belen, New Mexico
37" x 45"

Gecko-Mania
Harriet Smith, Albuquerque, New Mexico
38" x 38"

Ring Around The Rosie
Anita McSorley, Albuquerque, New Mexico
19" x 19"

Under A Blanket of Stars
Susie Gray, Tijeras, New Mexico
99" x 99"

UNDER A BLANKET OF STARS

By Susie Gray
99" x 99"

Susie selected a batik Pima cotton print for the background fabric in this quilt. Although beautiful, Pima cotton has little stretch because of the tight weave of the threads. She recommends using Pima cotton in

YARDAGE

3/4 yd. Total of three different
    light fabrics
2 yds. Total of seven different
    medium fabrics
1-1/2 yds. Total of four different
    dark fabrics
4 yds. Background
1-1/2 yds. Inner windowpane and
    border (mustard)
3 yds. Outer windowpane and
    triangle border (purple)
3-1/4 yds. Sashing and borders
    (blue)
1-1/4 yds. Inner triangle border
    (pink)
8-7/8 yds. Backing
1 yd. Binding

the blocks, not as background.

CUTTING - Cut the following sashing and border pieces and set aside.

Inner Windowpane and Border
  Twenty-eight 1" strips
  Eight 2" strips

Outer Windowpane and Outer Triangle Border
  Twenty-eight 2" strips
  Three 9-3/4" strips, into
    (10) 9-3/4" squares

Sashing and Borders
  Four 2-1/2" strips (windowpane)
  Four 4-1/2" strips, into
    (8) 4-1/2" x 16-1/2"
  Seven 4-1/2" strips
  Ten 4" strips

Inner Triangle Border
  Two 9-3/4" strips, into
    (8) 9-3/4" squares
  Two 2-1/2" strips, into

    (8) 2-1/2" x 8-1/2"
Background
  Two 19-1/16" strips, into
    (4) 19-1/16" squares

STAR BLOCKS

1. Make twelve 12-1/2" star blocks.

2. Stitch a double row of windowpane sashing to each block using the 1" and the 2" strips. The block should be 16-1/2".

CENTER STAR

Cutting
  Template A - cut 4 plus 4(r)
  Template B - cut 4 plus 4(r)
  Template C - cut 8
  Template D - cut 8 plus 8(r)
  Template E - cut 8 plus 8(r)
  Template F - cut 4 background

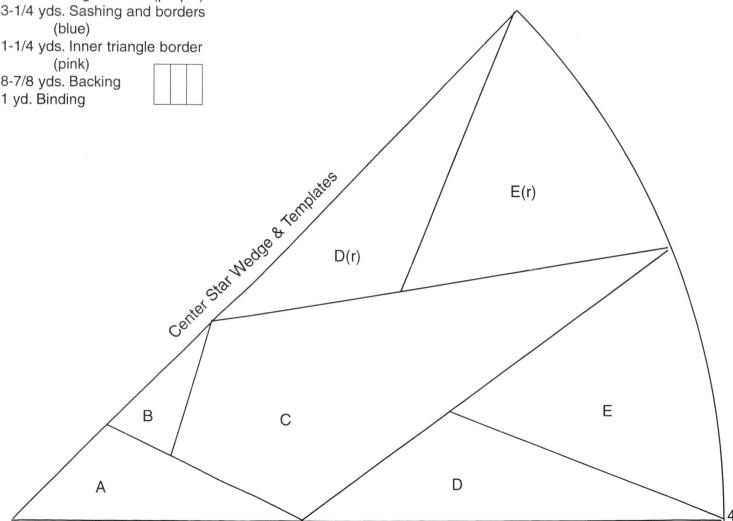

Center Star Wedge & Templates

A B C D E D(r) E(r)

Piecing

1. Stitch B to C.
Press seam toward C.

2. Stitch D to E and D(r) to E(r).
Press seam toward E.

3. Stitch DE to BC and D(r)E(r) to BC. Press seam toward E.

4. Stitch A to BC.
Press seam toward A.

5. Make four wedges like this plus four mirror-image wedges.

6. Stitch two wedges together to form a quarter circle. Stitch these together to form half circles. Stitch the half circles together.

7. Piece the background square F, page 43. Set the circular star into it. The block should measure 16-1/2".

8. Border the block with a triple row of windowpane sashing. Use 1" first, 2" second, and 2-1/2" third. The block should measure 24-1/2".

ASSEMBLY

Center Section - See quilt diagram, page 43.

1. Decide on the block arrangement. Eight star blocks plus the center star are used in the center. The other four star blocks are used in the corners.

2. The center section is stitched together in rows. To make the center row stitch a 4-1/2" x 16-1/2" sashing strip to the top and bottom of the two blocks on each side of the center star. Press seams toward the sashing. Sew these two blocks to the sides of the center star. Press seams toward the sashing.

3. For the top and bottom rows sew three blocks together with a sashing strip between the blocks. Use the four remaining 4-1/2" x 16-1/2"

42

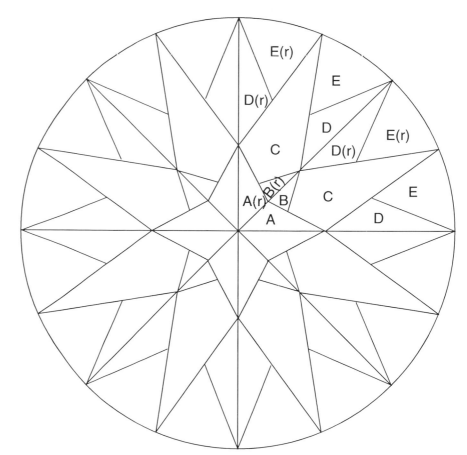

strips. Stitch one row above and one below the center row.

4. Sew together 4-1/2" border strips to make four 68" lengths. Sew one to each side of this center section, starting and stopping 1/4" from each edge. Miter the corners and trim the excess fabric.

Corner Triangles
5. Cut the 19-1/16" squares in half diagonally.

They need to have a corner trimmed before using. Lay the triangles on the cutting mat with the 90° corner at the top. Mark a point 1-7/8" from the right tip on four pieces and from the left tip on four pieces. Draw a line from this point which is perpendicular to the bottom edge. Cut along this line.

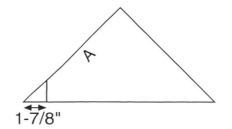

1-7/8"

Stitch this side "A" of the triangles to two sides of the remaining four corner blocks, starting and stopping 1/4" from the cut off corner. Stitch this seam at the corner of the blocks.

Triangle Border
6. Cut the 9-3/4" squares in fourths diagonally.

Stitch four inner triangles to five outer triangles. Stitch a 2-1/2" x 8-1/2" corner strip to the left side of four of the triangle border strips and to the right side of the remaining four border strips. Trim even with the top and bottom edge of the triangle border strips.

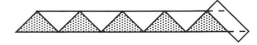

7. Stitch a 2" border strip to the inside edge of the triangle border. Press seams toward the 2" strip. Trim the excess fabric to form a

continuous line following that of the triangle border.

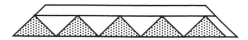

8. Stitch the triangle border to the outside edge of the corner triangles, stopping 1/4" from the corner. Do not miter the corners yet!

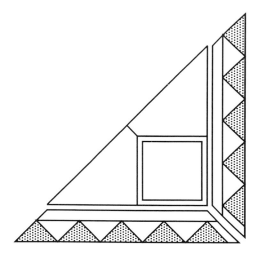

9. Stitch the corner triangles to the center section of the quilt top. Now the center is "on point!"

10. Piece the 4" border strips together to make four 104" lengths. Sew them to the triangle border, having at least 5" extend beyond the ends of the triangle border. Stitch. Press seams toward the 4" border. Trim the excess fabric so that the outer border continues the angle of the triangle border on the ends.

11. Stitch the mitered corner through all three borders.

The quilt top is complete - a true Blanket of Stars. Refer to page 12 for finishing.

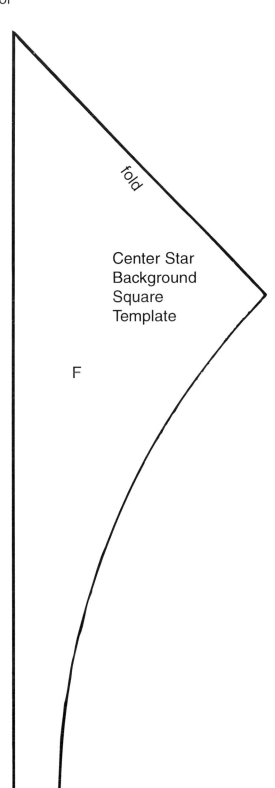

fold

Center Star
Background
Square
Template

F

OH MY STARS!

By Linnie Hyde
90" x 90"

Linnie learned to love the challenge of designing something herself and bringing it to fruition. She designed three of the 12" stars and the large center star in her quilt.

YARDAGE

1/4 yd. Each of 3-5 fabrics for stars
1/2 yd. Center star background (light purple)
1/2 yd. Center star border (dark teal)
3/4 yd. First inner border (light lavender)
3/4 yd. Second inner border (medium lavender)
1/2 yd. Third inner border (medium teal)
2 yds. Fourth inner and feathered borders (dark floral)
3 yds. Fifth inner border and small star background (burgundy)
1-1/2 yds. Large background triangles (tie-dye)
1 yd. Feathered border (medium aqua)
8-1/8 yds. Backing
1 yd. Binding

CUTTING - Cut the following pieces first. The remaining fabric is used to piece the stars.

Center Star Border
Four 2-1/4" strips

First Inner Border
Four 3-3/4" strips, into
(8) 3-3/4" x 21"

Second Inner Border
Four 3-1/4" strips, into
(8) strips 3-1/4" x 21"

Third Inner Border
Six 2-1/8" strips

Fourth Inner Border and Feathered Border
Six 3" strips
*Six 2-7/8" strips, into
(84) 2-7/8" squares
One 2-1/2" strip, into
(16) 2-1/2" squares

Fifth Inner Border
Six 2" strips
(64) background square pieces, page 14.

Large Background Triangles
One 18-1/4" strip, into
(2) 18-1/4" squares
One 9-3/8" strip, into
(4) 9-3/8" squares

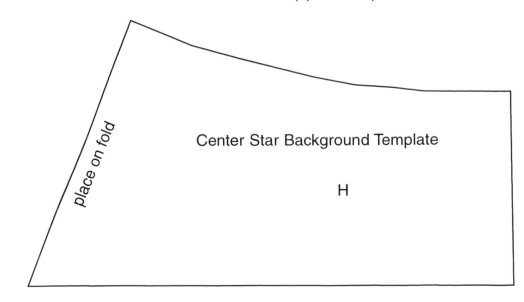

place on fold

Center Star Background Template

H

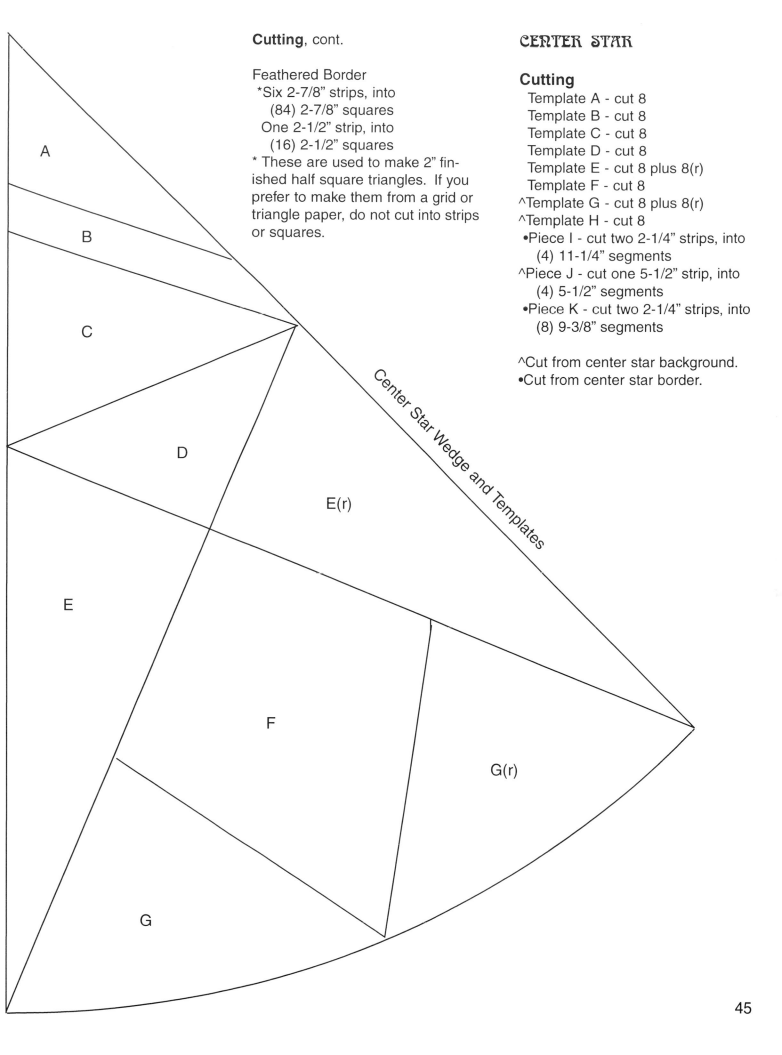

Cutting, cont.

Feathered Border
 *Six 2-7/8" strips, into
   (84) 2-7/8" squares
 One 2-1/2" strip, into
   (16) 2-1/2" squares
* These are used to make 2" finished half square triangles. If you
prefer to make them from a grid or
triangle paper, do not cut into strips
or squares.

A

B

C

D

E(r)

E

F

G(r)

G

Center Star Wedge and Templates

CENTER STAR

Cutting
  Template A - cut 8
  Template B - cut 8
  Template C - cut 8
  Template D - cut 8
  Template E - cut 8 plus 8(r)
  Template F - cut 8
 ^Template G - cut 8 plus 8(r)
 ^Template H - cut 8
 •Piece I - cut two 2-1/4" strips, into
     (4) 11-1/4" segments
 ^Piece J - cut one 5-1/2" strip, into
     (4) 5-1/2" segments
 •Piece K - cut two 2-1/4" strips, into
     (8) 9-3/8" segments

 ^Cut from center star background.
 •Cut from center star border.

45

Piecing

1. Stitch A to B to C.
Press seams away from B.

2. Stitch G to one side of F. Press seam toward G. Stitch G(r) to the opposite side of F. Press seam toward G(r).

3. Stitch E to FG.
Press seam toward FG.

4. Stitch E(r) to D.
Press seam toward D.

5. Stitch ED to EFG.
Press seam toward EFG.

6. Stitch ABC to DEFG.

7. Make eight wedges like this. Stitch two wedges together to form a quarter circle. Stitch the quarter circles together to form a half circle. Stitch the half circles together.

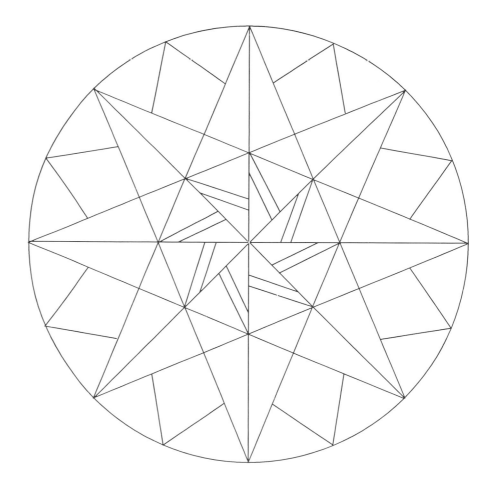

Refer to the quilt diagram, page 44, as you add the frames on this center section.

8. Stitch the H pieces together to form a background octagon. Set the circular star into the background octagon the same as setting it into a background square.

9. Cut mirror-image 45° angles from the ends of the I pieces.

Cut the J pieces in half, diagonally.

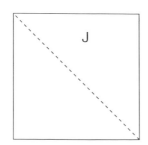

Stitch the long side of four J's each to the shorter long side of an I. Press seams toward the darker fabric. Stitch these pieces to every other side of the octagon to form a square.

10. Attach the 2-1/4" center star border as you would a single windowpane. The square should measure 28-1/4".

11. Cut mirror-image 45° angles from the ends of the K pieces just as done in step 9. Stitch a K to each short side of the remaining J pieces, stopping 1/4" from the point where the K's meet. Miter the K's.

12. Stitch the first and second inner border strips together. Trim one end of each to a 45° angle, cutting four from one end and four from the opposite end.

13. Sew these strips to the K units along the 45° edge. Sew to the sides of the center star and miter the corners.

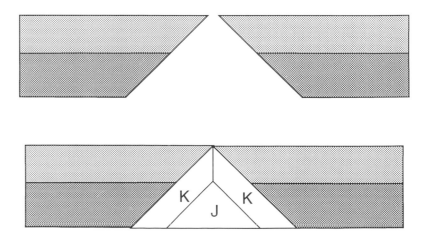

Inner Borders

Stitch the third, fourth and fifth inner border strips together to make four 53" lengths of each. Sew together and stitch to the center star as windowpane sashing. This section should measure 51-1/2".

Star Blocks

1. Make sixteen 12-1/2" star blocks.

2. Set them into the background squares cut previously.

Feathered Border

1. Place a medium 2-7/8" square on a 2-7/8" dark square. Draw a diagonal line connecting opposite corners. Stitch 1/4" on both sides of the line. Cut on the line. Repeat using all but four of each color square. OR make 160 half square triangles (2" finished) using the method you prefer.

2. Cut the 18-1/4" squares in fourths diagonally. Cut the 9-3/8" squares and the remaining 2-7/8" squares in half diagonally.

3. Using the star blocks, the pieces from steps 1 and 2, and 2-1/2" medium and dark squares, stitch the side feathered borders. Make four.

Stitch these borders to each side of the center quilt section.

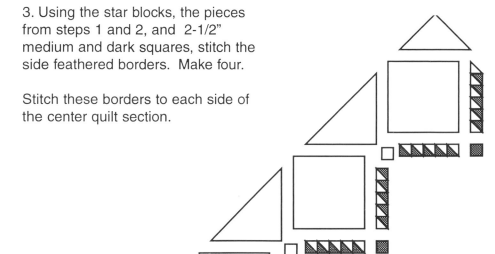

Side Border

4. Sew the borders on the corner blocks.

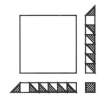

Stitch these into the corners, pivoting at the outer edge.

Binding

1. After quilting, bind the quilt using short binding strips. Press the strips in half lengthwise. Center and sew them to the edges of the quilt, starting and stopping at the seam lines.

2. Miter the outward pointing corners like a regular quilt corner.

3. The inside corners are mitered the same with one exception. When marking and sewing the miter have the point go away from the end of the strip, not toward it. These corners are either 135° or 90°.

4. Fold the binding to the back of the quilt and stitch down.

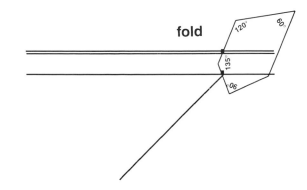

STAR STUDDED COMPASS

By Janet Wolfe
80" x 88"

Encouragement from Janet's husband to create a brown tone quilt determined the colors of Star Studded Compass. In an effort to find a mathematical formula for the ellipse, the setting for the quilt developed with the central elongated star.

YARDAGE

1/3 yd. Each of 8-10 fabrics for stars
4 yds. Background
2 yds. Narrow windowpane and middle border (green)
2 yds. Wide windowpane and large compass points (brown)
3/4 yd. Inner border and center star (peach)
1-1/4 yds. Outer border (rust)
5-1/3 yds. Backing
7/8 yd. Binding

CUTTING - First cut the large background pieces, windowpane sashing, and borders. The remaining is used to piece the stars.

Background
  (4) 26-1/4" x 13-3/4"
  (4) 9-3/4" x 17"
  (4) 2-1/2" x 16"

Narrow Windowpane
  (24) 1" strips
  (9) 2" strips

Wide Windowpane
  (16) 1-3/4" strips

Inner Border
  (9) 1" strips

Outer Border
  (9) 4-1/2" strips

STAR BLOCKS
1. Make eight 12-1/2" star blocks.

2. Frame four of the star blocks with a double border of windowpane sashing using 1" and 1-3/4" strips. These blocks measure 16".

3. Frame the remaining four blocks with a triple border of windowpane sashing using 1", 1-3/4", and 1" strips. These blocks measure 17".

CENTER COMPASS - This compass is designed to be pieced in concentric circles. There are four sections; each one is pieced separately. Each section, except for the outermost, forms a circle. Refer to the drawing below and on page 49 when piecing. Templates are on pages 49 - 53.

1. Stitch A to B. Press seams toward B. Make eight. Stitch together two wedges to form quarter circles. Press the seams in one consistent direction. Stitch these together to make half circles. Stitch the half circles together to complete the inner star.

2. Stitch E to one side of D, leaving 1/4" unstitched at the outermost point of D. This enables you to pivot at this corner. Stitch E(r) to the remaining side of D, again leaving 1/4" unstitched. Stitch E and E(r) together to complete this wedge. Press seams toward the background fabric. Make four wedges. Stitch C to one side of each wedge. Stitch the wedges together to complete this section. Either applique the inner star to this section or set it in with curve seam piecing.

3. Stitch F to G to H. Press seams away from G. Make 18 units. Stitch the units together to form a circle. Applique or piece the section from step 2 to this circle.

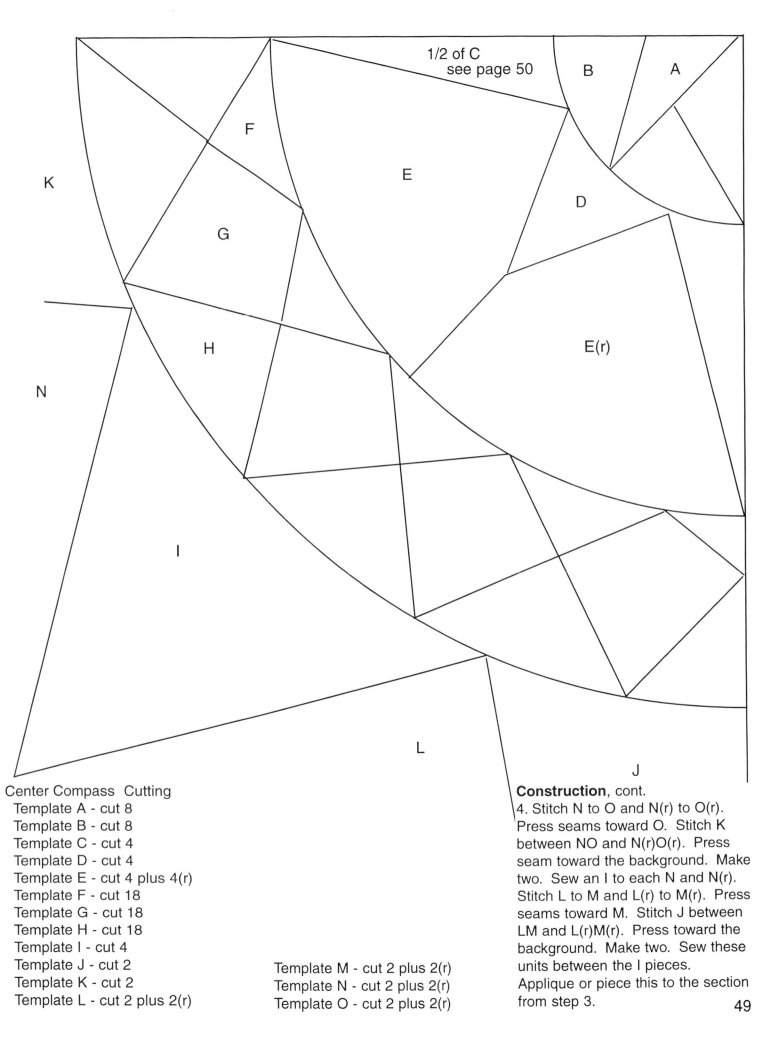

1/2 of C
see page 50

B   A

F

K   E

G   D

H   E(r)

N

I

L   J

Center Compass Cutting
  Template A - cut 8
  Template B - cut 8
  Template C - cut 4
  Template D - cut 4
  Template E - cut 4 plus 4(r)
  Template F - cut 18
  Template G - cut 18
  Template H - cut 18
  Template I - cut 4
  Template J - cut 2
  Template K - cut 2
  Template L - cut 2 plus 2(r)

  Template M - cut 2 plus 2(r)
  Template N - cut 2 plus 2(r)
  Template O - cut 2 plus 2(r)

Construction, cont.
4. Stitch N to O and N(r) to O(r).
Press seams toward O. Stitch K
between NO and N(r)O(r). Press
seam toward the background. Make
two. Sew an I to each N and N(r).
Stitch L to M and L(r) to M(r). Press
seams toward M. Stitch J between
LM and L(r)M(r). Press toward the
background. Make two. Sew these
units between the I pieces.
Applique or piece this to the section
from step 3.

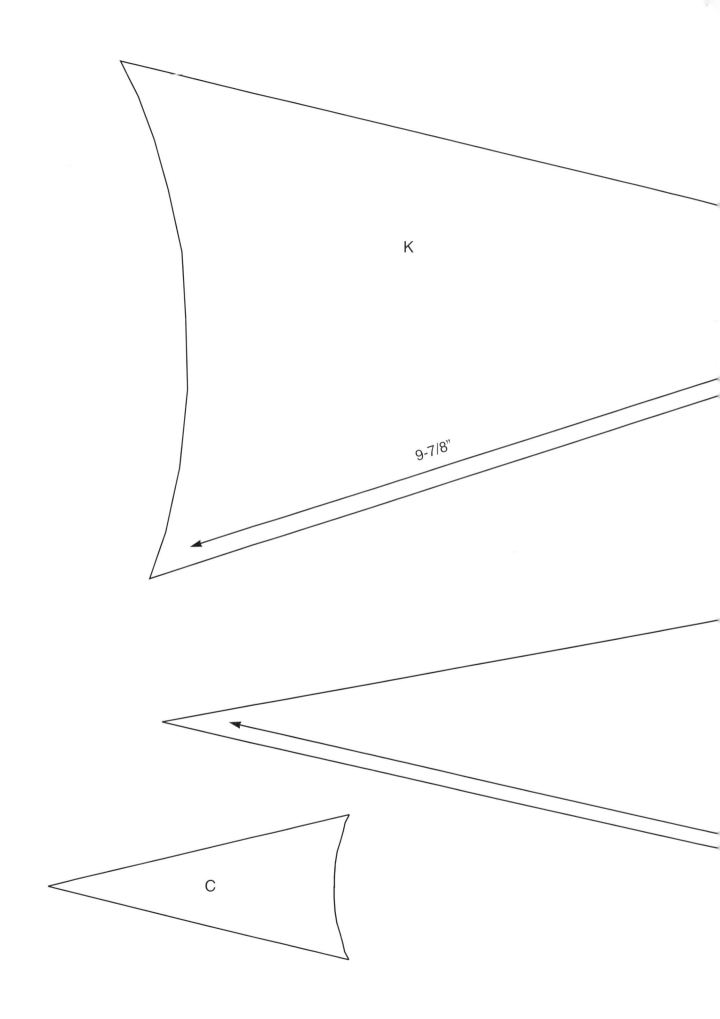

K

9-7|8"

C

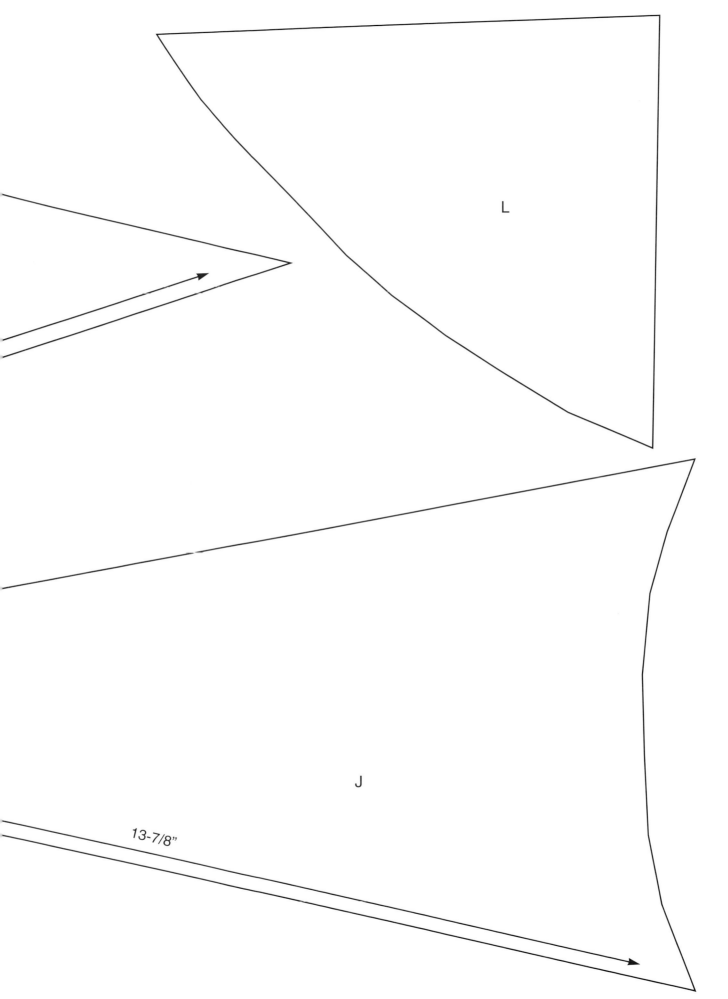

L

J

13-7/8"

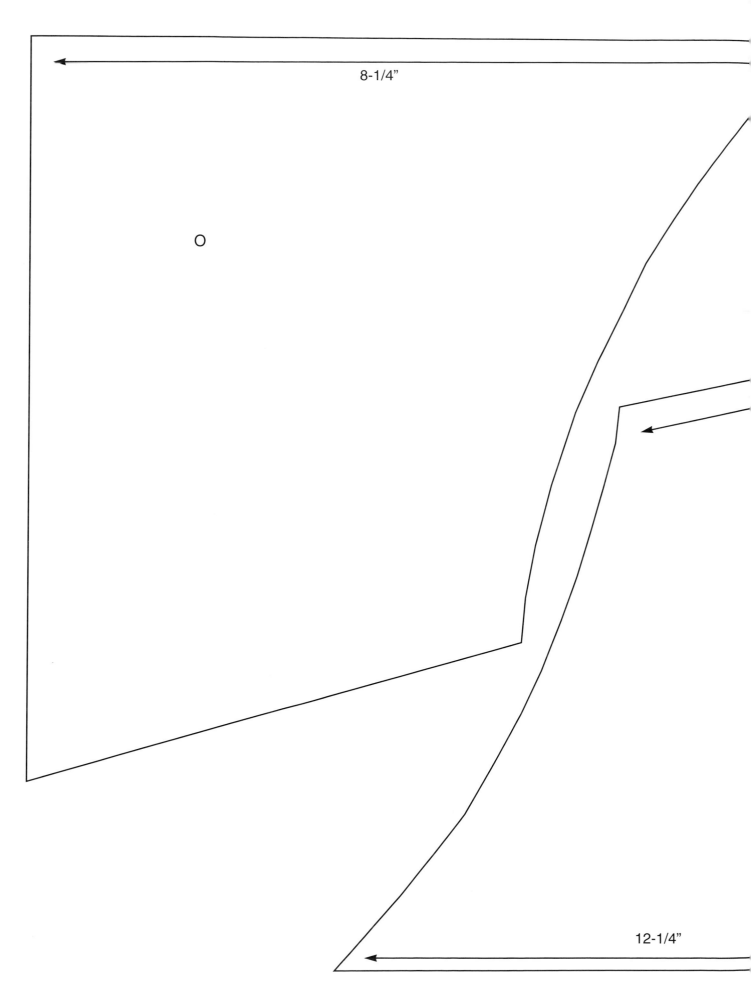

8-1/4"

O

12-1/4"

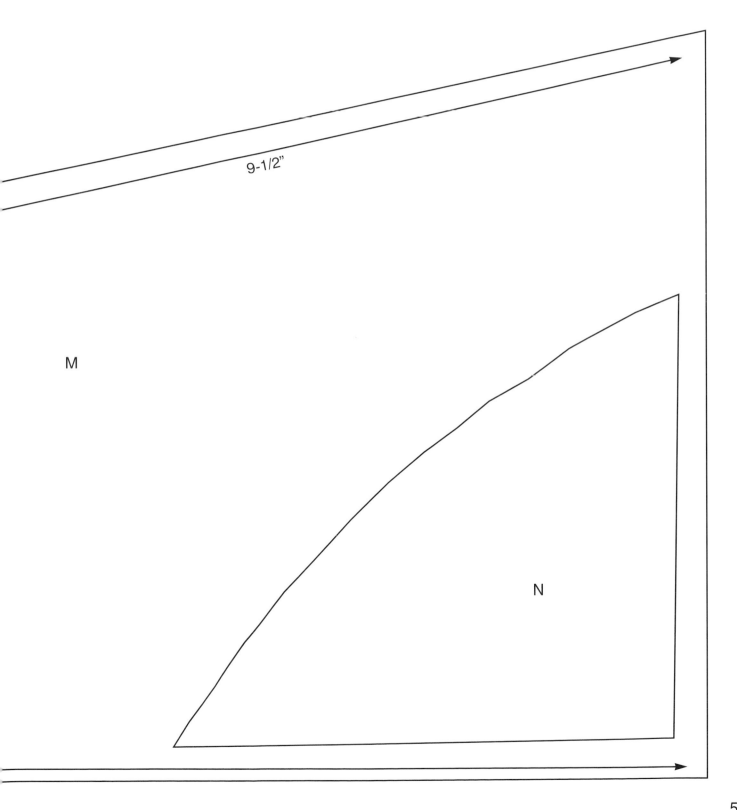

9-1/2"

M

N

ASSEMBLY

1. Stitch a block with a double windowpane sashing to each outer point of the compass. Stitch a 2-1/2" x 16" background to the end of each of these blocks.

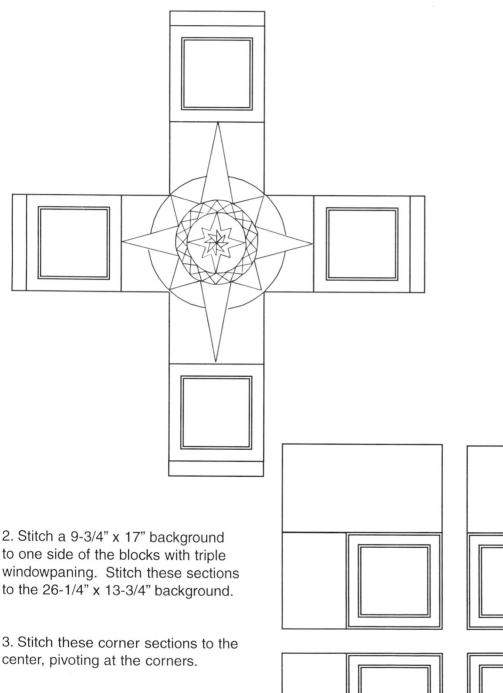

2. Stitch a 9-3/4" x 17" background to one side of the blocks with triple windowpaning. Stitch these sections to the 26-1/4" x 13-3/4" background.

3. Stitch these corner sections to the center, pivoting at the corners.

BORDERS

1. Piece the border strips to make two 82" and two 91" lengths of each border. Sew these long strips into sets of 1", 2", and 4-1/2".

2. Attach the border strip sets to the quilt like windowpane sashing.

STAR RADIANCE

By Helen Duncan
89" X 89"

Helen wanted to arrange her blocks in a circular set similar to one she had seen.

YARDAGE

4 yds.*Total of three light
  background
3 yds. Background of center star,
  windowpane and final border
  (burgundy)
2 yds. Feathers (dark green)
1 yd. Large star (medium green)
1 yd. Windowpane (medium green)
3/4 yd. Border (paisley)
2 yds. Total assorted prints for stars
3 yds. Backing
7/8 yd. Binding

*Include at least 2 yds. of one for
feathers and border and 3/4 yd. of
another for windowpaning if you
want to use the same print in these
areas.

CUTTING - Cut the following first
then set aside. Remaining fabric
may be used in piecing the stars.

Borders
First - Eight 2" x 22-1/2" strips
  (background)
Second - Eight 2-3/4" x 27" strips
  (paisley)
Final - Eight 5-1/2" x 45-1/2" strips
  (burgundy)

Windowpane Sashing
First - Sixteen 1" strips
  (background or med. green)
Second - Sixteen 1-3/4" strips
  (background or med. green)
Third - Sixteen 2" strips (burgundy)

*NOTE: Some of the following pieces
are similar in size. Label the pieces
as you cut them to avoid confusion.*

Feathered Eight-Pointed Star
Piece H - cut one 9" square
  (burgundy)

Piece I - cut two 14" strips
  (large star), into
  (8) 9-7/8" segments
Piece J - cut one 4-5/16" strip
  (feathers), into
  (8) 4-5/16" squares
Piece K - cut three 4" strips (back
  ground) and three 4" strips
  (feathers), into
  (24) 4-11/16" segments each
Piece L - cut one 4-11/16" strip
  (background), into
  (8) 4-11/16" squares
Piece M - cut two 4-5/16" strips
  (feathers)

Feathered Border
Piece N - cut one 4-7/8" strip
  (background) and one 4-7/8"
  strip (feathers), into
  (4) 4-7/8" squares
Piece O - cut one 4-7/8" strip
  (background) and one 4-7/8"
  strip (feathers), into
  (4) 4-3/4" segments each
Piece P - cut three 4-7/8" strips
  (background) and three
  4-7/8" strips (feathers), into
  (24) 4-5/8" segments each

Star Blocks
1. Make eight 12-1/2" star blocks.
Helen used different backgrounds in
her stars.

2. Attach a triple border of windowpane sashing using the strips cut
and the directions on page 10. The
blocks should measure 19".

Radiance Star, page 56
1. Stitch A to B to C.
Press seam away from B.

2. Stitch D to ABC.
Press seam away from D.

3. Stitch E to F.
Press seam toward F.

4. Stitch EF to ABCD.
Press seam toward EF.

5. Make four wedges like this plus
four mirror-image wedges.

6. Stitch a wedge to a mirror-image
wedge to form a quarter of the block.
Stitch two of these together to make
a half block. Stitch two half blocks
together to complete the star.
9. Add G to complete the corners of
the square. It fits the short outer
section of the block (where the
longest points touch the outside
edge.) The block should be 19".

Assembly

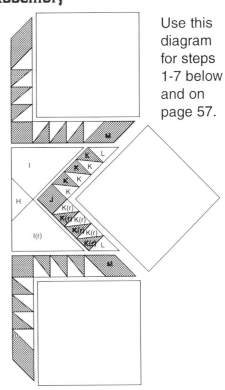

Use this
diagram
for steps
1-7 below
and on
page 57.

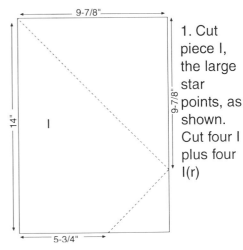

1. Cut
piece I,
the large
star
points, as
shown.
Cut four I
plus four
I(r)

Cut piece H into quarters diagonally.

Stitch I and I(r) to the short
sides of H. Press seams
away from H. Make four.

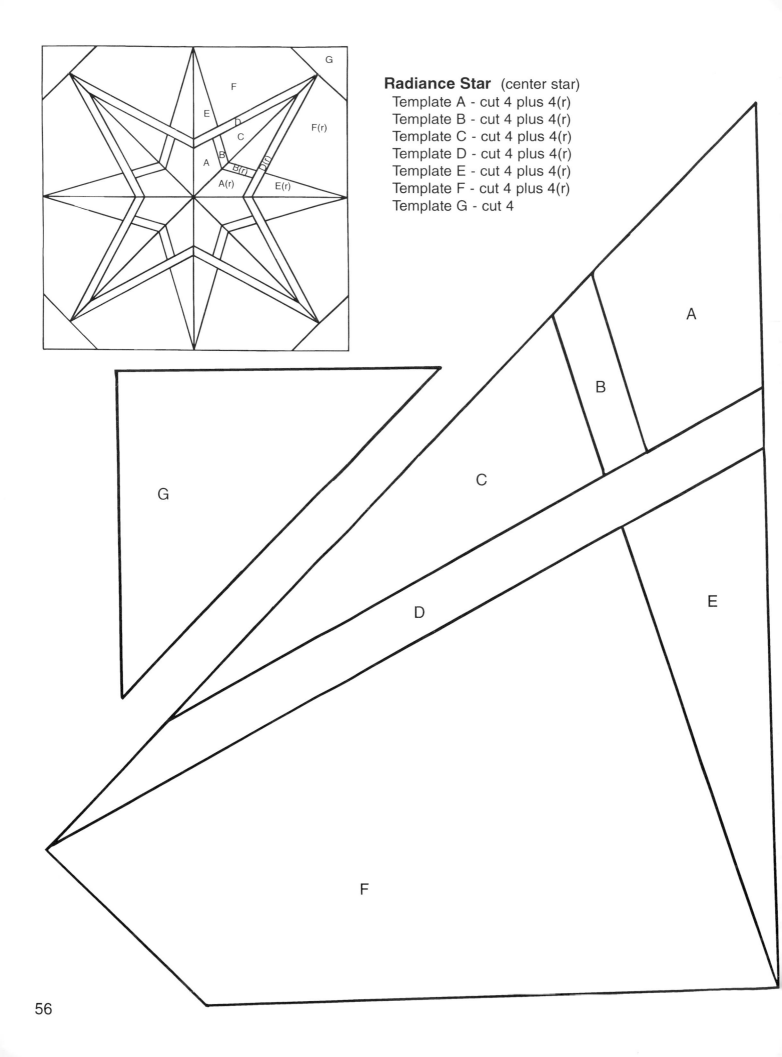

Radiance Star (center star)
Template A - cut 4 plus 4(r)
Template B - cut 4 plus 4(r)
Template C - cut 4 plus 4(r)
Template D - cut 4 plus 4(r)
Template E - cut 4 plus 4(r)
Template F - cut 4 plus 4(r)
Template G - cut 4

2. Cut piece K in half diagonally. Cut half of each color as shown at left, half as at right.

Stitch feathers K to background K and feathers K(r) to the background K(r). Press seams toward the green. This forms rectangles K and K(r). Make 24 of each.

3. Cut piece L in half diagonally.

Using pieces J, rectangles K and K(r), and L, stitch a feather unit. One side of the unit uses K while the other side uses K(r). Be sure to sew these together along the longer side of K and K(r). Make eight.

4. Stitch four of these units to HI, pivoting at the center. Stitch two of these to opposite sides of Radiance Star.

5. Cut the strip for M into diamonds. Cut a 45° angle at one end of the strips. Cut eight 4-3/8" segments.

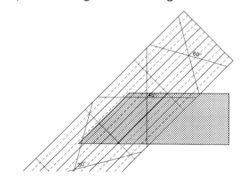

Add M to the remaining four feather units. Sew these to the side of the two units left from step 4.

6. Stitch these to the remaining sides of Radiance Star.

7. Set an 19" star block between each of the points, pivoting at the center.

Borders

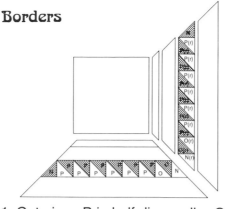

1. Cut piece P in half diagonally. Cut half of each color as shown at left, half as at right.

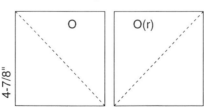

Stitch feathers P to background P and feathers P(r) to background P(r). Make 24 of each.

2. Cut piece O in half diagonally. Cut half of each color as shown at left, half as at right.

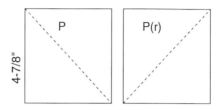

Stitch feathers O to background O and feathers O(r) to background O(r). Make four of each.

3. Cut piece N in half diagonally. Cut half of each color as shown at left, half as at right.

Stitch the P units and O units together as shown, along the longer sides. Sew N and N(r) on the ends.

4. Center each 2" border strip on a 2-3/4" border strip and sew together. Center these on the narrow (inside) edge of the feathered borders and stitch. Press seams away from the feathered border. Use a ruler with a 45° angle to trim the inner border so it aligns with the feathered border on both sides.

5. Stitch the 5-1/2" borders to the opposite side of the feathered borders as described in step 4.

6. Stitch these border sections to the star blocks, pivoting at the point of the diamond in the inner feathered star.

7. Miter the corners of the quilt to complete the top.

STARRY, STARRY NIGHT

By Gail Garber
78" x 78"

In making this quilt, I was inspired by a view of the night sky through the imaginary window of my mind. Each star is individually framed in an off-set windowpane. I used two shades of black for the background, a star print for the area behind the windows, and a matte, tone-on-tone for the center Mariner's Compass and the borders.

YARDAGE

2-1/4 yds. Background #1 (starry black)
3 yds. Background #2 (matte black)
1 yd. Each of eight different solid colors ranging in color value from light to dark
1-1/4 yds. Outer windowpane (swirl stripe)
1 yd. Binding (also used in blocks)
5 yds. Backing

CUTTING

Background #1
  Four 8" strips, into
    (8) 8" x 15-1/2" rectangles
    (4) 8" squares
  Six 2" strips, into
    (4) 2" squares, remainder for border
  Use the remainder for the background of the twelve stars.

Background #2
  One 8" strip, into
    (4) 8" squares
    (8) 2" x 8" rectangles
  Template G - cut 40 plus 40(r)
  Template I - cut 40 plus 40(r)
  Template K - cut 40 plus 40(r)
  Use the remainder for the background of the center Mariner's Compass.

Select three color values; a light, medium, and dark, from the solid color fabrics. From these cut:
  Template H - cut 40 dark
  Template L - cut 40 medium
  Template J - cut 40 light

Use four color values for the inner windowpane pieces. (templates are "dashed lines", pages 60-61)
  Template M - cut 8 dark
  Template M(r) - cut 8 medium dark
  Template N - cut 8 light
  Template N(r) - cut 8 medium light

Outer windowpane
  Template O - cut 32

STAR BLOCKS

Make eight 12-1/2" star blocks. Trim each block to measure 12", for a 11-1/2" finished block size.

WINDOWPANE SASHING

Templates, pages 60 and 61
Caution - Sew the inner and outer windowpane sashing on in two steps.

1. Stitch the inner sashing (M and N) to the star blocks. Miter the corners. Press seams to the side of least resistance.

2. Sew on the outer sashing (O) and miter the corners.

MARINER'S COMPASS CENTER

Drawing and templates, page 59

This block is stitched together in wedges which are then stitched to the center circle. This particular design lends itself to isolating prints, especially in the center. This compass has two sets of points. One set of points appears to be in front of the other. Select the most dominant fabric for these points to accentuate the illusion.

TIP - Make split points of the compass using two different fabrics. Measure the width across the widest part of the compass point. Divide this measurement in half and add seam allowances. Cut two different strips of fabric this wide, and stitch together into a strip set. Cut the templates from the two-colored strip, centering the template on the seam line.

Cutting

Template A - cut 8
Template B - cut 8
Template C - cut 8
Template D - cut 8
Template E - cut 16 from background #2
Template F - cut 4 plus 4(r) from background #2

Piecing

1. Stitch E to D. Press seam toward E. Stitch E to the other side of D. Press seam toward E.

2. Stitch B to C as illustrated in the piecing diagram. Press seam toward C.

3. Stitch DE to BC. Press seam toward DE. Make eight wedges.

4. Stitch the eight wedges together to form a circle. There will be a hole in the center.

5. Stitch A pieces together into pairs to form quarter circles. Press seams consistently in the same direction. Stitch these into half circles; then stitch the half circles together.

6. Applique the center to the circle from step 4, matching the seams of the center to the inner points of piece C.

7. Stitch the background pieces F, page 60, together. Sew the circular compass into the background square.

BORDER BLOCKS

Templates, page 61

A simple, 7-1/2" block (finished size) is used to create both the border around the compass block and the outer border. Make 40 of these blocks.

1. Stitch I to H. Press seam toward I. Stitch I(r) to H. Press seam toward I(r).

2. Stitch K to J. Press seam toward K. Stitch K(r) to J. Press seam toward K(r).

3. Stitch HI to KJ. Press seam toward KJ.

4. Stitch HIJK to L. Press seam toward L. You now have a large triangle.

5. Stitch G to one side of the large triangle. Press seam toward G. Stitch G(r) to the other side of the triangle. Press seam toward G(r).

ASSEMBLING THE QUILT TOP

Refer to the assembly diagram to stitch the top together. Use the 8" background #1 pieces as fillers. If you look carefully at the central portion of the scale drawing, you will notice some areas which can be stitched together into rows.

BORDERS

Inner Border

1. Stitch the 2" background #1 strips together end to end. Measure the quilt and cut borders. Sew borders to both sides of the quilt. Press seams toward the border.

2. Sew a 2" square to each end of the top and bottom borders. Press seams toward the borders. Stitch to the top and bottom of the quilt.

Outer Border - Refer to the drawing on page 60 for assembly of outer borders.

3. Stitch eight border blocks together as illustrated. Make four border strips.

4. Stitch a 2" x 8" background #2 rectangle to each end of the border strips.

5. Stitch an outer border to both sides of the quilt. Press seams toward the inner border.

6. Stitch an 8" background #2 square to each end of the remaining borders. Press seams toward the square.

7. Stitch the top and bottom borders in place.

Your quilt top is complete! Finish by layering and quilting your top as described on page 13.

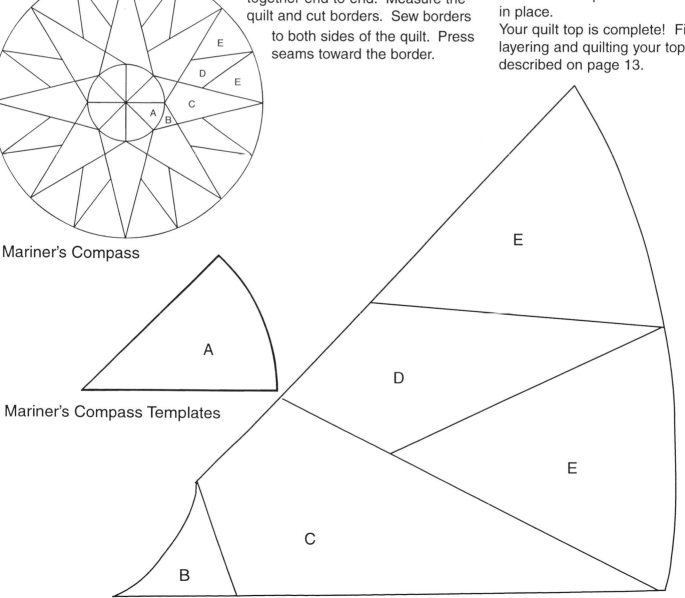

Mariner's Compass

Mariner's Compass Templates

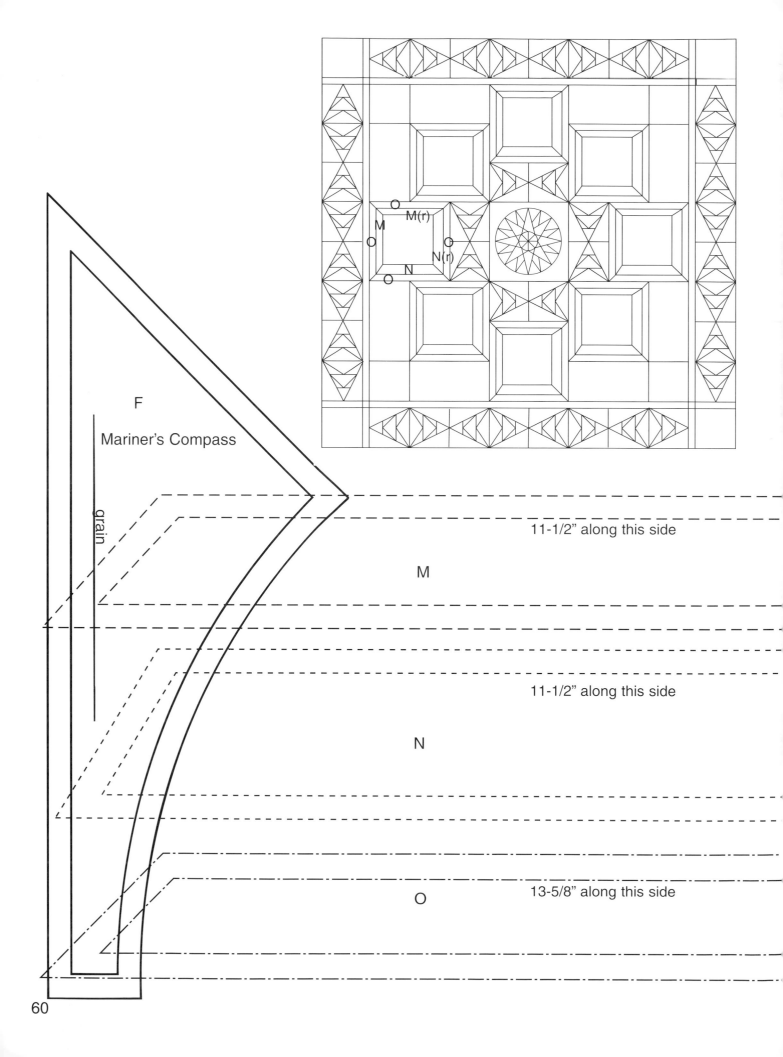

F

Mariner's Compass

grain

11-1/2" along this side

M

11-1/2" along this side

N

13-5/8" along this side

O

M(r)

M

O

N(r)

N

O

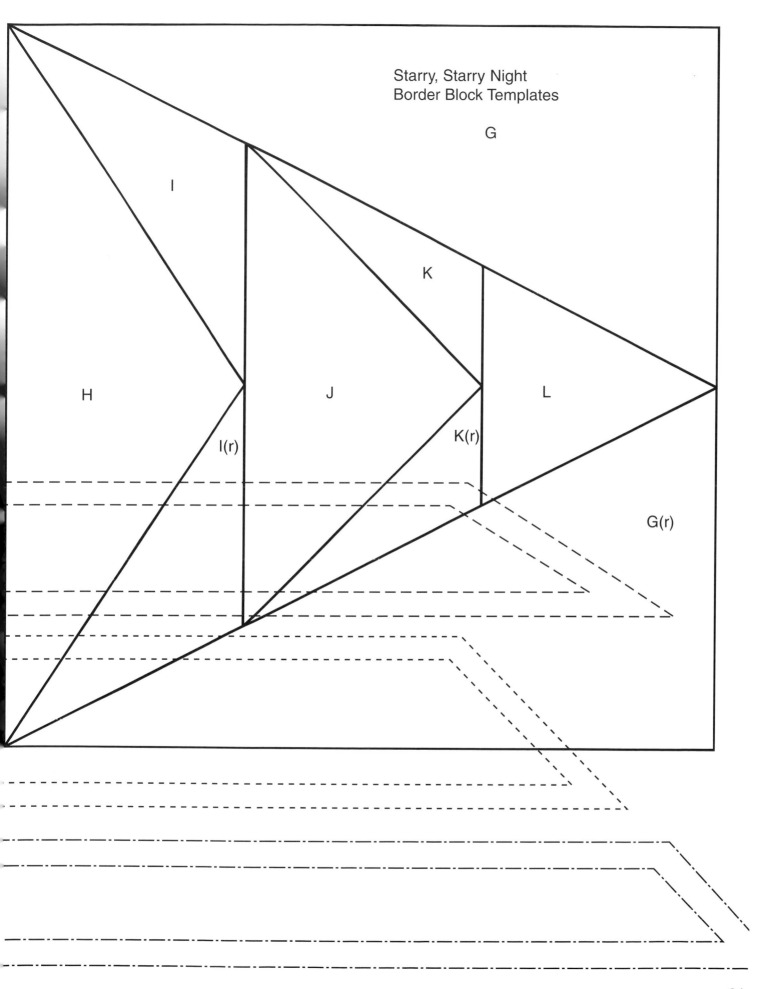

Starry, Starry Night
Border Block Templates

G

I

K

H

J

L

I(r)

K(r)

G(r)

STARS IN MY GARDEN

By Darlene Jones
105" x 96"

YARDAGE

1/2 yd. Each 4-6 fabrics for stars
2/3 yd. Background center star (pink)
5 yds. Main (floral)
3-1/2 yds. Light windowpane and
   border, background small
   stars, (pink)
2-1/2 yds. Medium windowpane and
   border (teal)
2-1/2 yds. Dark windowpane and
   border (forest green)
8-5/8 yds. Backing
1 yd.   Binding

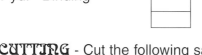

CUTTING - Cut the following sashing and border pieces and set aside. Remaining fabric is used to piece the stars.

Main
  Windowpane
    (4) 1-1/4" strips
  Sashing
    (8) 4-1/2" strips, into
      (4) 4-1/2" x 31-1/2"
      (8) 4-1/2" x 17-1/2"
      (4) 4-1/2" squares
    (10) 2-1/2" strips, into
      (8) 2-1/2 x 23-1/2"
      (16) 2-1/2" x 9-1/2"
      (16) 2-1/2" squares
  Sashing Stars
    (2) 5-1/4" strips, into
    (32) 2-5/8" x 5-1/4"
  Borders
    (8) 4" strips
    (10) 2-1/2" strips

Light
  Windowpane
    (22) 1-1/2" strips, into
      (24) 1-1/2" x 18"
      (4) 1-1/2" x 14"
      (8) 1-1/2" x 33"
      (4) 1-1/4" strips
  Borders
    (8) 2-1/2" strips

Medium
  Windowpane
    (24) 1-1/2" strips, into
      (12) 1-1/2" x 33
      (24) 1-1/2" x 18"
  Borders
    (8) 3-1/2" strips

Dark
  Windowpane
    (23) 1" strips, into
      (4) 1" x 33"
      (16) 1" x 18"
      (32) 1" x 14"
  Sashing Stars
    (2) 5-1/4" strips, into
      (32) 2-5/8" x 5-1/4"
  Borders
    (8) 1-1/2" strips

Garden Star (center star)
  Template A - cut 4 plus 4(r)
  Template B - cut 4 plus 4(r)
  Template C - cut 4 plus 4(r)
  Template D - cut 4 plus 4(r)
  Template E - cut 4 plus 4(r)
  Template F - cut 4 plus 4(r)
  Template G - cut 4 plus 4(r)
  Template H - cut 4 plus 4(r)

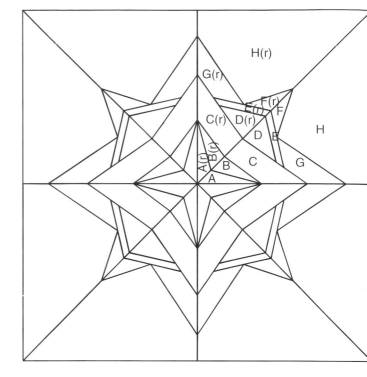

Garden Star

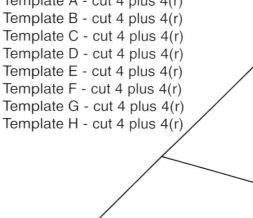

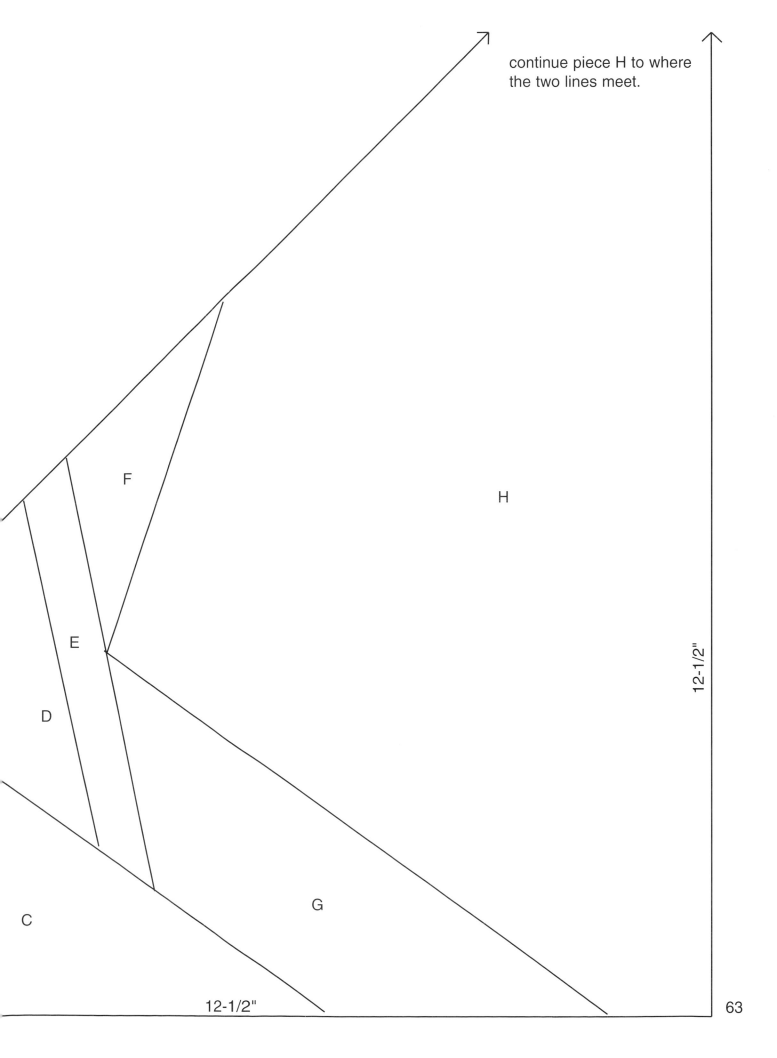

continue piece H to where the two lines meet.

F

H

E

D

C

G

12-1/2"

12-1/2"

STAR BLOCKS

1. Make twelve 12-1/2" star blocks.

2. Sew a triple row of windowpane sashing around four of the blocks. Use the 1" dark, 1-1/2" light, and 1-1/2" medium windowpane strips. The blocks are 17-1/2".

3. Sew a 1" dark windowpane around the remaining blocks. Sew them into pairs with a 1-1/2" pink strip between. Border these rectangles with a double windowpane of 1-1/2" pink and 1-1/2" teal. They are 17-1/2" x 31-1/2"

GARDEN STAR - Templates, pg. 63

1. Stitch F to H. Press seams toward H. Stitch G to H. Press seams toward H.

2. Stitch D to E. Press seams toward D.

3. Stitch DE to FGH. Press seams toward DE.

4. Stitch A to B to C. Press seams away from B.

5. Stitch ABC to DEFGH.

6. Make four wedges like this plus four mirror-image wedges. Sew the wedges together to make a 25-1/2" block.

7. Sew on four rows of windowpane sashing using 1" dark, 1-1/4" light, 1-1/2" medium, and 1-1/4" main strips. The block is now 31-1/2".

SASHING

1. Cut the 2-5/8" x 5-1/4" main and dark pieces in half diagonally. Stitch a dark triangle to a main triangle. Press seams toward the dark. Make 64.

2. Stitch a sashing rectangle, step 1, to each end of a 2-1/2" x 9-1/2" sashing strip. Make 16.

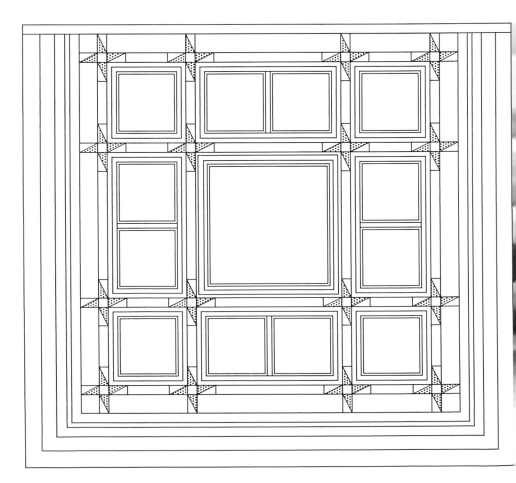

64

3. Stitch a sashing rectangle to each end of a 2-1/2" x 23-1/2" sashing strip. Make 8.

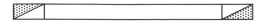

Refer to the quilt diagram as you assemble the sashing rows and the quilt, steps 4 - 9 below.

4. Make each long sashing row with two short sashing strips, step 2, one long sashing strip, step 3, and four 2-1/2" squares. Make 4.

5. Each outer border of the sashing is made with four sashing rectangles, two 4-1/2" x 17-1/2" main sashing strips, and one 4-1/2" x 31-1/2" main sashing strips. Make two rows with a 4-1/2" square at each end and two rows without.

6. Assemble the quilt in horizontal rows. Make the center row by stitching a long sashing strip, step 3, to opposite sides of Garden Star. Sew a two-block rectangle to each side. Add long sashing strips to the outside edges of the row.

7. Make the top and bottom rows by sewing together a star block, a two-block rectangle and a star block, with short sashing strips, step 2, between and on the ends.

8. Stitch the rows together with a long sashing row, step 4, between each set of blocks and on the top and bottom.

9. Stitch a border strip without the 4-1/2" squares, step 5, to opposite sides of the quilt top. Sew the remaining two strips to the top and bottom.

BORDERS

1. Piece the border strips to make one 107" and two 94" lengths of each. Make three long strip sets of 2-1/2" main, 1-1/2" dark, 2-1/2" light, 3-1/2" medium and 4" main. Attach the borders to the sides and the bottom like windowpane sashing, page 10.

2. Piece 2-1/2" main strips to make one 107" length. Sew to the top of the quilt.

CIRCUS OF THE STARS

By Gail Garber
62" x 80"

A whimsical collection of primary colors from a line of fabric by Virginia Robertson was the inspiration for this quilt.

YARDAGE

1/4 yd. Each of 8 - 10 different fabrics (primary colors) for individual blocks.
1-1/2 yds. Background (blue sky)
1/4 yd. Inner windowpane sashing (dark blue print)
1-1/2 yds. Outer windowpane (red/blue print)
yds. Sashing and blocks (light floral print)
1-7/8 yds. Outer borders and binding (red print)
4-7/8 yds. Backing

CUTTING

Inner Windowpane
(24) 1" strips

Outer Windowpane
(24) 2" strips

Sashing
(34) 1-1/4" strips

Outer Borders and Binding
(7) 2-3/4" strips
(20) 1-1/4" strips
(7) 2-1/2"

STAR BLOCKS

Make twelve 12-1/2" star blocks. Use the leftover fabrics from above, the blue sky background, and the primary colors to piece the blocks.

WINDOWPANE SASHING

Stitch the 1" strips to the 2" strips. Attach the windowpane sashing as directed on page 10. The blocks are now 16-1/2".

NINE PATCH SASHING

1. Use 1-1/4" strips to make sixteen strip sets of light floral, red, light floral. Press seams toward the middle. Cut (31) 16-1/2" segments.

2. Use 1-1/4" strips to make two strip sets of red, light floral, red. Press seams outward. Cut (44) 1-1/4" segments.

Use the leftover strip sets from step 1 and cut (28) 1-1/4" segments.

Piece (20) nine-patch blocks with red outer corners. These are used in the sashing.

Piece (4) nine-patch blocks with light outer corners. These are used for the corners.

3. Sew the blocks into horizontal rows with a sashing piece between blocks and on the ends of the rows.
4. Stitch the sashing pieces and nine-patch blocks together into five rows.

5. Stitch the rows together with sashing rows between.

OUTER BORDER

Cut top, bottom and side borders. Sew the top and bottom borders to the quilt top. Press seams toward the border. Stitch a nine-patch block to each end of the side borders. Stitch the side borders to the quilt top. Press seams toward the border.

The top is done. Refer to finishing, page 12, for ideas on how to complete your quilt.

PEEK-A-BOO STARS

By Janet Wolfe
78" x 79"

Peek-a-Boo Stars' coloration evolved from an extraordinary fabric that signaled to Janet from the shelf. Setting the stars together in an asymmetrical design allowed only limited space for additional stars – hence the stars peek around the corners. It's very easy to make; pay attention to the scale drawing.

YARDAGE

1/3 yd. Each of 10 assorted (stars)
1/4 yd. Each of light and medium
    (peek-a-boo stars)
2-1/2 yds. Background
1/3 yd. Inner windowpane
2-1/8 yds. Main windowpane and
    narrow border
1-1/8 yds. Wide border
4-3/4 yds. Backing
3/4 yd. Binding

CUTTING

Background - Cut or piece as needed to make lengths
  Eight 3-3/4" strips, into
    (1) 3-3/4" x 57-1/4"
    (1) 3-3/4" x 51-3/4"
    (1) 3-3/4" x 17-1/2"
    (5) 3-3/4" x 15-1/2"
    (5) 3-3/4" x 12-1/4"
    (4) 3-3/4" x 9"
    (2) 3-3/4" x 5-3/4"

  Two 5-3/4" strips, into
    (1) 5-3/4" x 46-3/4"

  Two 7" strips, into
    (1) 7" x 43-1/2"

  One 2-1/2" strip, into
    (1) 2-1/2" x 15-1/2"

Inner Windowpane
  (4) 2-1/8" strips

Main Windowpane and
Narrow Border
  (18) 2" strips
  (16) 2" strips

Wide Border
  (8) 4-1/2" strips

Peek-a-Boo Stars
  Template A - cut 45 medium and
      5 light
  Template A(r) - cut 36 light and
      4 medium
  Template B - cut 40 background
  Template C - cut 10 background
  Template D - cut 30 background

STAR BLOCKS

1. Make nine 12-1/2" stars. Border seven of the stars with a single 2" windowpane, page 10. The blocks should be 15-1/2".

2. Attach a double windowpane sashing to the remaining two stars, using both the 2" and 2-1/8" sashing. The blocks should measure 18-3/4".

PEEK-A-BOO STARS - There are nine mostly medium stars and one mostly light star. Make the mostly medium stars as directed below then make the mostly light, reversing the light and medium pieces. The block is only 3/4 of a star, so it will fit around a corner of the large star blocks.

1. Stitch A to A(r), starting and stopping 1/4" from each edge (this enables you to pivot at the corners). Press seam toward the medium fabric. There will be one medium A left over from each star.

2. Set in the background B, pivoting at the inside corner. Press seam toward the background fabric.

3. Stitch the leftover A to background C. Press seam toward the background.

4. Stitch the five sections of the star together to form a 3/4 circle.
5. Stitch three background D pieces together. Set the circular star into the background, page 10.

TIP - Each time a peek-a-boo star is stitched to the corner of a block, it will be necessary to pivot at the corner.

ASSEMBLY

1. Refer to the scale drawing for the correct positioning of the background pieces. Following the diagram, stitch sections together which can then be stitched to the bordered star blocks.

2. See the color photograph, page 33, for borders. Sew the 2" border strips in pairs along the selvage to make eight long (approximately 80") strips. Do the same with the 4-1/2" border strips, making four long strips. Make four long strip sets of 2" border, 4-1/2" border, 2" border. Attach the borders to the quilt top like windowpane sashing, page 10.

The top is done. Refer to the finishing section for ideas on how to complete your quilt.

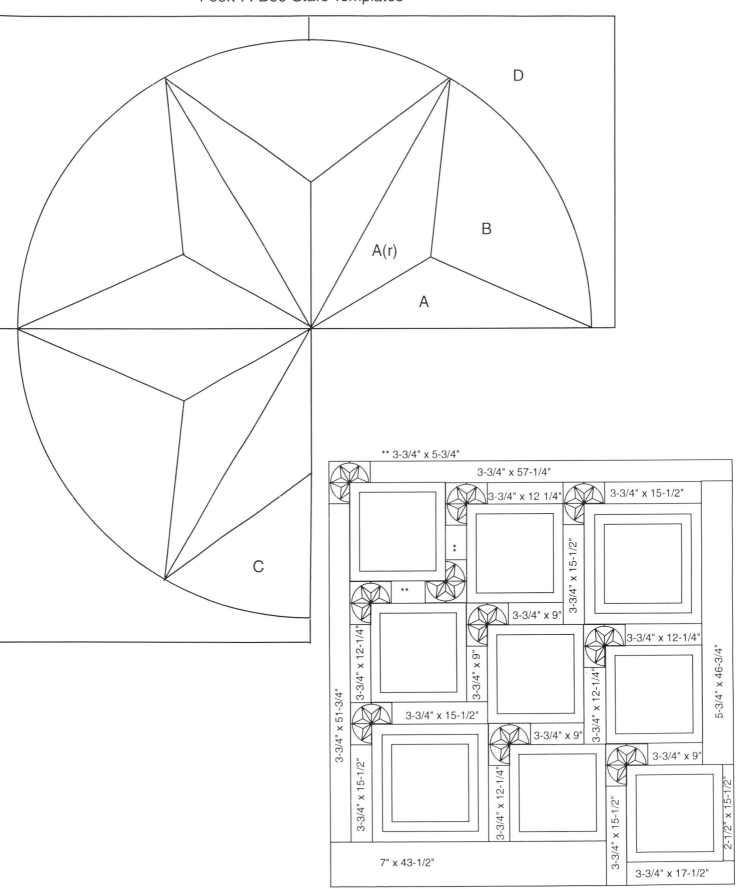

A VIEW FROM SANDI'S WINDOW

By Sharon Johnson
37" x45"

Sharon's oldest daughter, Sandi, and her Dad have spent untold hours star-gazing at all hours of the night. As Sandi prepares to leave home, Sharon wanted to create for her a memento to keep those memories alive.

YARDAGE

1-1/2 yds. Background (blue)
1/4 yd. Side border (Light brown)
1/8 yd. Top border (medium brown)
1/2 yd. Outer border and binding (dark brown)
1/8 yd. Each of 6-8 different fabrics for stars
1-1/2 yds. Backing
1/2 yd. Binding

CUTTING

Background
  One rectangle 19-1/2" x 5-1/2"
  One rectangle 12" x 16"
  Two rectangles 2" x 12"
  Two rectangles 3" x 12"
  One rectangle 3-1/2" x 5-1/2"

Borders
  Sides - two 3-1/2" strips
  Top - two 2" strips
  Outer - five 2-1/2" strips

STAR BLOCKS

Make five 12-1/2" star blocks of your choice. Trim the blocks to 12" for a finished size of 11-1/2". Sharon included the two original blocks, Star In a Square, page 30, and Spinning Star, below.

SPINNING STAR – 5-1/2"
finished star

Cutting
  Cut five of each template A, B, C, and D.
  Cut four of template E.

Piecing

1. Stitch B to C.
Press seam toward C.

2. Stitch BC to D.
Press seam toward D.

3. Stitch A to BCD.
Press seam away from A.

4. Make five wedges like this.

5. Stitch wedges together into pairs. Stitch the remaining wedge to one of the pairs. Stop and backstitch 1/4" from each center point.

6. Stitch the two-wedge unit to the three-wedge unit, pivoting at the center.

7. Make the background square (E) and set the star into it as explained on page 10.

ASSEMBLY

1. Refer to the quilt diagram, below right, to assemble the quilt top. If you look carefully you will notice that there are four horizontal rows in the quilt.

2. Applique the free-form star, page 69, to the upper right hand square.

BORDERS

1. Stitch side border strips to each side of the quilt top, stopping and starting 1/4" from the upper edge of the quilt. Leave extra fabric at the top for mitering. (Notice that the lower edge is finished straight across and is not mitered.)

2. Stitch the top border strip to the top of the quilt, starting and stopping 1/4" from the edge.

3. Miter the top corners. Because the borders are not the same size the miter will not be a 45° corner. On the side borders measure 1-3/4" beyond the end of the border seam line and make a mark on the ouside edge of the side border. Draw a line from the end of the seam line to this mark for the miter stitching line. Prepeat this process with the top border, except mark the outer edge of the border 3-1/4" beyond the seam line. Align the seam lines and stitch the miter. Trim excess fabric.

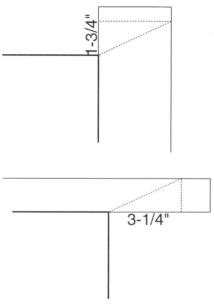

4. Add the outer border as you would a single row of windowpane sashing.

The top is complete.

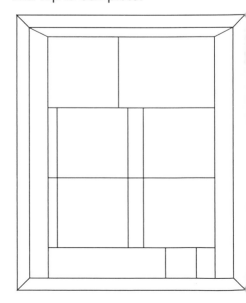

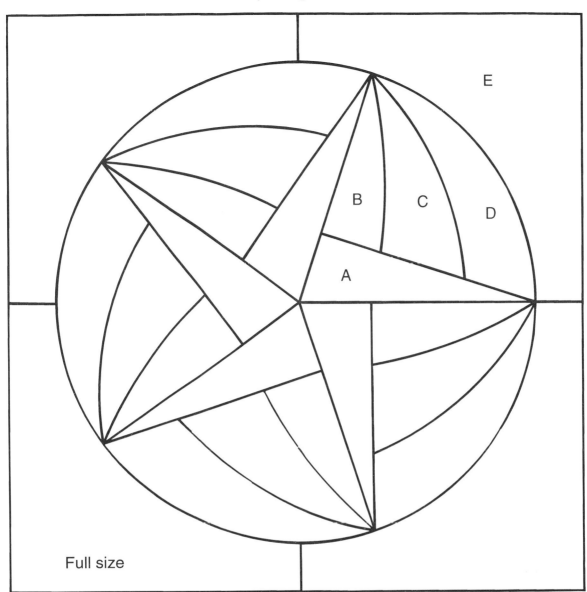

E

B   C

D

A

Full size

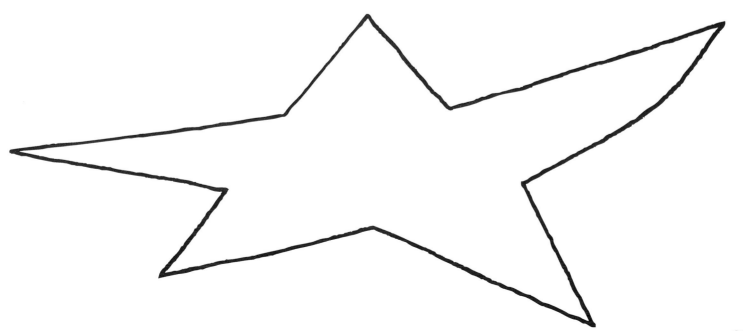

RING AROUND THE ROSIE

By Anita McSorley
19" x 19"

The name of this little quilt defines the geometric rose-like center encircled by a ring, and, of course, the color selected. Anita chose to work with only two fabrics, a print used in the outer border and Color Bars® by EZ International. This fabric shades from light to dark within one piece.

YARDAGE
1-1/2 yds. Color Bars® or 1/8 yd. each of seven shades from light to dark
1/3 yd. Border and binding
5/8 yd. Backing

CUTTING
Label the fabrics from #1 to #7, with #1 the lightest and #7 the darkest. This helps keep the colors separate during the cutting process.

Template A - Cut 4 plus 4(r) from #3
Template B - Cut 8 from #1 and 8 from #2
Template C - Cut 4 plus 4(r) from #6
Template D - Cut 8 from #4 and 8 from #5
Template E - Cut 4 plus 4(r) from #7
Template F - Cut 4 plus 4(r) from #1
Template G - Cut 4 from #6
Template H - Cut 4 From #3

Border
  Two 2-1/4" strips

PIECING
1. Stitch F to E.
Press seam toward F.

2. Stitch D (#4) to E.
Press seam toward D.

3. Stitch C to D (#5).
Press seam toward C.

4. Stitch B (#1) to C.
Press seam toward C.

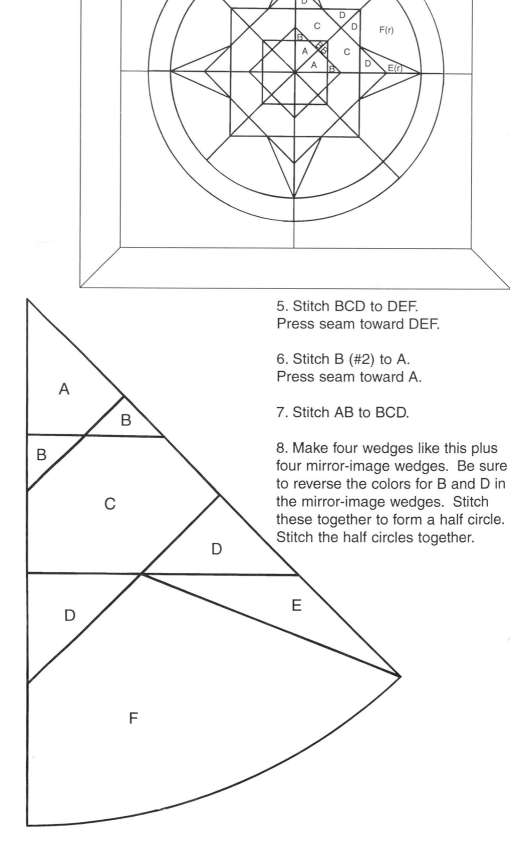

5. Stitch BCD to DEF.
Press seam toward DEF.

6. Stitch B (#2) to A.
Press seam toward A.

7. Stitch AB to BCD.

8. Make four wedges like this plus four mirror-image wedges. Be sure to reverse the colors for B and D in the mirror-image wedges. Stitch these together to form a half circle. Stitch the half circles together.

70

Stitch two wedges together to form quarter circles.

0. Stitch the four G pieces together to form a circle. Set the circular star into the ring.

1 Sew the background pieces (H) together and sew to the star as explained on page 10.

2. Stitch 2-1/4" border strips to each side of the quilt, stopping 1/4" from each end. Miter the corners.

G

H

Add 1/4" seam
allowance
at this end.

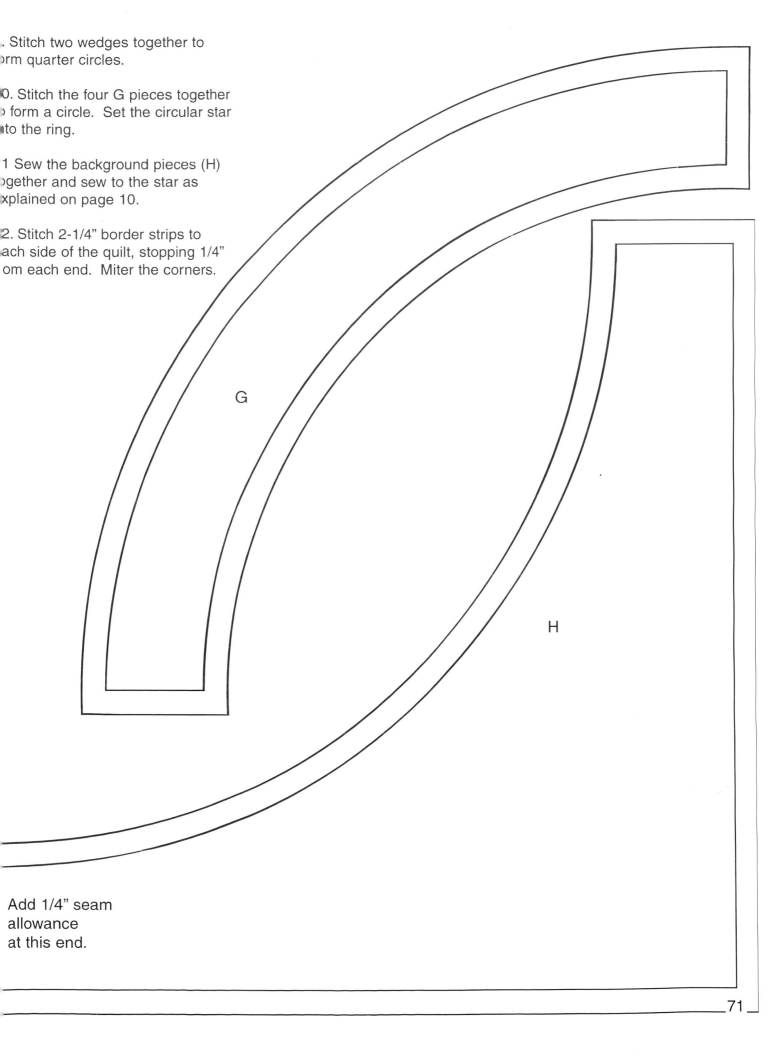

Other books by ANIMAS QUILTS PUBLISHING

WEAVER FEVER by Jackie Robinson — $ 6.50
Bargello type quilts in a woven design. Easy.

QUADCENTRICS by Jackie Robinson — $ 7.00
Designs which travel over and under each other.

TESSELLATIONS by Jackie Robinson — $ 12.00
Geometric shapes forming a repeating pattern.
Inspired by M.C. Escher.

ON THE DOUBLE by Suzan Drury — $ 14.00
Two-for-one quilts cut from one basic strip set.

DINING DAZZLE by Jackie Robinson — $ 16.00
A collection of 20 placemats and 4 table runners.

REFLECTIONS by Melinda Malone — $ 13.00
Positive-negative designs in great quilts.

SIMPLY LANDSCAPES by Judy Sisneros — $ 14.00
Turn your favorite scene into a quilt with ease.

APPLIQUE, THE EASY WAY — $ 20.00
by Kathryn Kuhn and Timmie Stewart
No basting or pressing with this easy method.

TAKE 2 by Joanna Myrick — $ 14.00
Eleven two-color quilts with complete directions.

STARBOUND by Susan Dillinger — $ 8.00
Coordinated treeskirts, stockings, table runners, etc.

CHILDREN'S ZOO by Barbara Morgan — $ 18.00
A safari of animals in quilts and accessories.

TERRIFIC TRIANGLES by Shelly Burge — $ 18.00
Slick tricks for scrappy half-square triangles.

QUILTS in the Tradition of FRANK LLOYD WRIGHT — $ 19.00
by Jackie Robinson. Based on art-glass windows.

EASY TRADITIONAL QUILTING by Lora Rocke — $ 15.00
Historic quilting designs presented in continuous form.

PERENNIAL PATCHWORK by Jackie Robinson — $ 11.00
A garden of flower blocks in eight different "sets".

STAR GAZING by Jackie Robinson — $ 12.00
Ohio stars in several variations.

CHAINS OF LOVE by Jackie Robinson — $ 10.00
Double and Triple Irish Chain quilts.

BINDING MITER TOOL — $ 4.00
Make mitered corners on quilt bindings
easy and perfect every time.

PLEASE ADD POSTAGE:

$ 1.75 FOR 1 ITEM
$ 2.50 FOR 2 - 4 ITEMS
$ 3.50 FOR 5 - 9 ITEMS

THANK YOU!

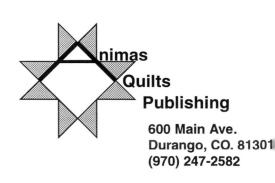

**Animas
Quilts
Publishing**

**600 Main Ave.
Durango, CO. 81301**
(970) 247-2582